T0156920

The Other Bible Code

Also by Val Pym

THE FALL OF THE GATES OF HELL

THE TRUE SABBATH [booklet]

The Other Bible Code

Unlocking the Glorious Destiny
of the Church of
Jesus Christ

VAL PYM

iUniverse, Inc.
New York Bloomington

The Other Bible Code
Unlocking the Glorious Destiny of the Church of Jesus Christ

Copyright © 2010 by Val Pym

All rights reserved. No part of this book may be used or reproduced by any means,
graphic, electronic, or mechanical, including photocopying, recording, taping or by
any information storage retrieval system without the written permission of the publisher
except in the case of brief quotations embodied in critical articles and reviews.

iUniverse books may be ordered through booksellers or by contacting:

iUniverse
1663 Liberty Drive
Bloomington, IN 47403
www.iuniverse.com
1-800-Authors (1-800-288-4677)

Because of the dynamic nature of the Internet, any Web addresses or links contained in this
book may have changed since publication and may no longer be valid. The views expressed
in this work are solely those of the author and do not necessarily reflect the views of the
publisher, and the publisher hereby disclaims any responsibility for them.

ISBN: 978-1-4502-4132-8 (sc)
ISBN: 978-1-4502-4133-5 (ebook)

Printed in the United States of America

iUniverse rev. date: 8/25/2010

All scripture quotations, unless otherwise indicated, are taken
from the New King James Version® Copyright © 1982 by Thomas
Nelson Inc.. Used by permission. All rights reserved.

Other quotes from The Amplified Bible © 1965 by Zondervan
Publishing House. Used by permission.

Edited by Debra Hughes Writer's Literary Agency

Dedicated to

THE AUTHOR AND FINISHER OF OUR FAITH

JESUS CHRIST

and for

my beloved husband

ROBBIE

"..an Israelite indeed, in whom is no guile" John 1:47

with appreciation for unfailing support

*"Blessed be the God and Father of our Lord Jesus Christ, who according to His abundant mercy has begotten us again to a living hope through the resurrection of Jesus Christ from the dead, to an inheritance incorruptible and undefiled and that does not fade away, reserved in heaven for you, who are kept by the power of God through faith and for salvation **ready to be revealed in the last time.**"*
1 Peter 1:3-5 emphasis added

"Our eyes are holden that we cannot see things that stare us in the face until the hour arrives when the mind is ripened. Then we behold them, and the time when we saw them not is like a dream"

Ralph Waldo Emerson

Preface

A few Words from the Author

Contrary to what some say, it matters a great deal what we believe concerning end-time events.

The Church is the channel through which God's will is accomplished in the Earth, therefore it is vital that we understand what that will is. Jesus said that the Holy Spirit would guide us into all truth and show us things to come so we need to be open to an ongoing revelation of the will and purposes of God

I am aware that the concepts contained herein will conflict with the popular end-time scenario; which view I also held for some years. However it is my prayer that the reader will approach this book with an open mind and invite the witness of the Holy Spirit Who is the Spirit of Truth.

The Church moves forward by revelation and it is my earnest hope that God will use this book in some measure to help to expand the vision of the Church that it may move with confidence into the great destiny He has planned.

I acknowledge with gratitude the many faithful people who nurtured me in the faith and encouraged and supported me in any way in my journey of faith. The Body of Christ is One, flowing together and reaching toward that time when

" ... we all come to the unity of the faith and the knowledge of the Son of God, to a perfect man, to the measure of the stature of the fullness of Christ." Ephesians 4:13

Contents

Chapter 1. A Dream of Restoration

God has a dream—a dream of an Earth filled with the knowledge of the Lord, a world without wars and hatred and all the ravages of sin, where the beauty and harmony of Eden are restored and man lives at peace with God and his fellow man. His dream will come to pass. From the time of the Fall of Man and the corruption of Creation, God has been at work to bring it about. Earth was meant to be an extension of Heaven and Jesus taught us to pray that God's Name shall be honored, His Will be done, and His Kingdom come on Earth as it is in Heaven. This prayer will be answered.

God is in the business of restoration. He restores our soul (Psalm 23:3), i.e., He brings us back to wholeness. He has made provision for the healing of our bodies. He restores relationships, bringing love and forgiveness into broken situations. One of the great promises that we can claim is found in Joel 2:25, *"I will restore to you the years that the locust has eaten."*

When God restores anything it is better than it ever was. When God restored Job, he received twice as much as he had ever had. In Zechariah 9:12 God says, *"Return to the stronghold, you prisoners of hope. Even today I declare that I will restore double to you."*

In the hands of God, nothing is beyond restoration. The time is coming when this sin-spoiled Earth will be cleansed, restored, and filled with the Glory of God. In Acts 3:19–21, we read that the heavens must retain Jesus, *"until the time of the <u>restoration of all things</u>, which God has spoken by the mouth of all His holy prophets since the world began"* (emphasis added).

Some might say that this means that when Jesus comes again He will restore all things. However, Jesus Himself said that the work of restoration involves the mysterious appearance of "Elijah." The disciples Peter, James, and John had been on the Mount of Transfiguration with Jesus. They had seen Him talking to Moses and Elijah and heard the voice from Heaven. Their minds must have turned to the prophecy at the close of the Old Testament Scriptures:

Behold I send you Elijah the prophet

Before the coming of the great and dreadful day of the Lord

And he will turn the hearts of the fathers to the children

And the hearts of the children to their fathers,

Lest I come and strike the earth with a curse. (Malachi 4:6)

This prophecy was kept before Israel at the annual Passover celebration when a cup of wine was placed on the table for Elijah in anticipation of his return. There were four cups of wine which were drunk in conjunction with four promises of deliverance. They were:

1. "I will take you out."
2. "I will save you."
3. "I will redeem you."
4. "I will take you as a nation."

There was a fifth promise, "I will take you into the Land," and a fifth cup which is never drunk. This is the cup of Elijah.

Even though Israel eventually possessed the Promised Land, they look for a greater deliverance which is yet to come. Elijah will herald the coming of the Messiah and they will possess the Land in peace. It was the promise of a golden age when Messiah would sit on the throne in Jerusalem and rule the Earth. When Elijah comes, they believe, he will explain fully the meaning of the fifth cup and all mysteries.

Seeing Elijah on the mountaintop and remembering the prophecy, the disciples must have thought that the day of the Messiah had come. When Jesus instructed them not to tell of the vision until after the resurrection, they asked, *"Why then do the scribes say that Elijah must come first?"*

Jesus replied, *"Elijah truly is coming first and will <u>restore all things</u>"* (Matthew 17:10, 11; emphasis added). He went on to say that Elijah had already come, referring to John the Baptist who came *"in the spirit and power of Elijah to turn the hearts of the fathers to the children, and the disobedient to the wisdom of the just to make ready a people prepared for the Lord"* (Luke 1:17).

John's appearance on the stage of history was a partial fulfillment of the prophecy. It was a sign that restoration had begun. The ministry of Elijah is not yet complete. At the time Jesus spoke, John was dead. Yet Jesus said that Elijah was still to come and would restore all things. Elijah was the great prophet of the Spirit in the Old Testament. By the anointing of the Spirit upon him, Elijah challenged the Prophets of Baal—satanic powers of darkness of the day—and turned the nation back to God. Jesus' reference to Elijah here is not the literal return of the Old Testament Prophet but the Spirit coming on human flesh to restore all things and prepare the way for the Second Coming of the Lord. *Elijah* will turn the world back to God.

The restoration of all things has already been accomplished in seed form at the Cross.

> *For it pleased the Father that in Him [Jesus] all the fullness should dwell, and by Him to <u>reconcile all things</u> to Himself, by Him, whether things on earth or things in heaven, having made peace through the blood of His cross. (Colossians 1:19, 20; emphasis added)*

The restoration of all things has already been accomplished in seed form at the Cross.

When Jesus said "It is finished," that work of reconciliation was completed. It is an accomplished fact in the realm of the Spirit. We can bind and loose on Earth that which is already bound and loosed in Heaven (or in the realm of the Spirit). Reconciliation becomes restoration in the Earth when it is claimed by faith, e.g., a sinner is born again by the Spirit of God when he believes that Jesus has died to reconcile him to God. That reconciliation was accomplished two thousand years ago but it has to be appropriated. So it is with all that was accomplished at the Cross.

God continues to bring restoration whenever and wherever faith is exercised. The greater the revelation of the reconciling work of the Cross that we have, the greater the measure of restoration will be. That's why it is crucial to have an ongoing vision. The reconciliation of all things will be manifested as the restoration of all things when *Elijah* comes, *Elijah* being the Spirit of God coming in fullness upon the people of God in these last days. The Holy Spirit continues to lead and guide us into all truth and reveal things to come to all who are open to receive. When *Elijah* comes, the Church will enter into all that Jesus accomplished at His first coming. All things will be restored and Jesus will return to take up His throne on Earth. All of creation is waiting for that time.

For the earnest expectation of the creation eagerly waits for the revealing of the sons of God. For the creation was subjected to futility, not willingly, but because of Him who subjected it in hope; because the creation itself also will be delivered from the bondage of corruption into the glorious liberty of the children of God. (Romans 8:19–21)

In Biblical history, we find that Creation reflects the spiritual state of man. The Fall corrupted all of nature. When wickedness increased on the Earth, it resulted in the Flood, which again radically changed the face of the Earth. It has been shown in the *Transformations* video series hosted by George Otis Jr. that when revival takes place, even the surrounding area is renewed, pollution and corruption recede and the Earth begins to flourish. The answer to the climate crisis the world faces is to change the spiritual climate of Planet Earth.

All of God's dealings with Man have been toward the Restoration. It is the message *"which God has spoken by the mouth of all His holy prophets since the world began"* (Acts 3:21). Restoration sometimes requires cleansing and chastening but the goal hasn't changed. In the face of all the chaos on Earth caused by Man's rebellion, God still wants the message of Restoration to be declared. In the following passage, we can sense something of the burden of God's heart when His servants don't deliver the message.

"Hear, you deaf; and look, you blind, that you may see.

Who is blind but My servant, or deaf as My messenger whom I send?

Who is blind as he who is perfect, and blind as the Lord's servant?

Seeing many things, but you do not observe; opening the ears, but he does not hear."

The Lord is well pleased for His righteousness' sake;

He will magnify the law and make it honorable.

But this is a people robbed and plundered; all of them are snared in holes,

And they are hidden in prison houses;

They are for prey, and no one delivers;

For plunder, and <u>no one says "Restore!"</u> (Isaiah 42:18–22; emphasis added)

We are living in a day in which, increasingly, the people are prey to all the snares and evil devices of our spiritual enemy. Captive of his deceit, plundered and robbed to build his anti-God kingdom, the world seems headed towards destruction. In the face of all this, God still wants the message of Restoration declared on Earth. The messengers see and hear many things, and there is much speculation, but there are not many saying "Restore." Mostly the message is "Retreat" (or, "Rapture at any moment"). Most messengers are preparing to abandon the Earth to the ravages of the enemy.

God gave His beloved Son to the Earth to be the means of restoration. Speaking prophetically of the One Who was to come, God said *"I will preserve You and give You as a covenant to the people, To restore the earth, to cause them to inherit the desolate heritages"* (Isaiah 49:8).

Jesus came to reconcile ALL things to God (Colossians 1:20). The full effects of the Cross are yet to be manifested in the Earth. The restoration of all things <u>will</u> come to pass. Meanwhile, wherever the people of God lay hold of the reconciling work of the Cross, the process of restoration continues: broken lives, broken families, even broken communities can experience restoration.

Chapter 2. Abraham, God's Representative

Since God has given custody of the Earth to man, and corruption came by man, restoration of the Earth must also come via man. In Psalm 115:16 we read that God has given the Earth to "the children of men." God works in the world only by the willing co-operation and faith of people. As we study the heroes of faith listed in Hebrews 11, we cannot fail to notice that God always required human channels in order to bring to pass His great and mighty deeds in the Earth. Faith is the switch which unleashes the power and purpose of God and releases it into the human situation.

God shared His dream of restoration with a man called Abram (later changed to "Abraham"). He is "the father of all those who believe" (Romans 4:11). Abraham became God's representative in the Earth. God promised Abraham a land which would belong to his descendants forever and that through them all the Earth would be blessed.

Abraham stood on a mountaintop in the Land of Promise. God told him,

> *"Lift up your eyes now and look from the place where you are—northward, southward, eastward and westward; for all the land which you see I give to you and your descendants*

forever...Arise, walk in the land through its length and its width, for I give it to you." (Genesis 13:14–17)

The Holy Spirit must have been there with the celestial binoculars that day, because Abraham saw a long way:

* He saw that the Land represented much more than just a bit of real estate.

* He saw the day of Christ.

"Your father Abraham rejoiced to see My day." (John 8:56)

* He saw that his spiritual descendants would inherit the Earth.

"For the promise that he would be <u>heir of the world</u> was not to Abraham or his seed through the law but through the righteousness of faith." (Romans 4:13; emphasis added)

* He saw that possession of the land would ultimately result in the City of God on Earth.

"...he sojourned in the land of promise as in a foreign country, dwelling in tents with Isaac and Jacob, the heirs with him of the same promise; for he waited for the city which has foundations, whose builder and maker is God." (Hebrews 11:9)

It was the Land of Promise and all the promises of God were contained in it.

If you were to stand on the Mountain of Faith, how far could you see? All Christians have seen that through the Cross they have been forgiven and they have eternal life. As marvelous as that is, it is only the land around the bottom of the mountain.

The farther up Faith Mountain you go, the more you can see, and what you see is yours to claim. We climb Faith Mountain by reading and believing the Word. As the old song says, *"Lord plant my feet on higher ground."* Can you see as far as Father Abraham saw? Can you see that the Earth is ours to possess? It is our inheritance—lost in Adam and regained in Christ. The spiritual Seed of Father Abraham is *"heir of the world."*

At the top of the mountain the view is cosmic. We can see that the reconciliation of all things on Earth and in Heaven, and the restoration of all things, are provided in the Cross. Martin Luther King on the night before he was assassinated said, *"Don't look at your present situation; look to the future. I have been to the mountaintop. I have seen the Promised Land. Mine eyes have seen the glory of the coming of the Lord."*

What did he see? What was the dream he had? Did he see, in part, something of God's dream of restoration? A world restored—the way God intended it to be?

God has one answer and one answer only, one remedy for a fallen world—the Cross of Jesus Christ—but it is more than sufficient. Every redemptive act of God in the Old Testament pointed to the Cross and all restoration flows from it. (See illustration.)

GOD'S ONLY ANSWER

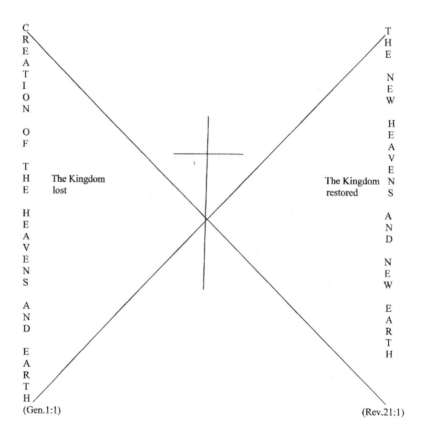

CREATION OF THE HEAVENS AND EARTH
(Gen.1:1)

The Kingdom lost

The Kingdom restored

THE NEW HEAVENS AND NEW EARTH
(Rev.21:1)

Every redemptive act of God in the Old Testament points to the Cross and all restoration flows from it.

It is a finished work, and nothing can be added to it. We have yet to discover and claim all that the Cross has brought. Most Christians believe that we enter into our inheritance when we die. However, the inheritance became ours when Jesus died.

> *He is the Mediator of the new covenant, by means of death, ...that those who are called may receive the promise of the eternal inheritance. For where there is a testament, there must also of necessity be the death of the testator. For a testament is in force after men are dead, since it has no power at all while the testator lives. (Hebrews 9:15–17)*

It is all ours now! But it has to be claimed.

Abraham walked the length and breadth of the Land and claimed it and all that it represented for himself and his descendants forever.

The Promised Son

The fulfillment of God's plan and His promise to Abraham hinged on the birth of a son and the surrender of that son to God. Through that son would come a people who would one day possess the promised inheritance and there establish the rule of God, i.e., the Kingdom. This son would bring blessing to the whole Earth. Through Abraham and his physical descendants, God demonstrated how restoration would come to the Earth.

In due time the promised son, Isaac, was born to Abraham and his wife Sarah in their old age. His birth was in itself a miracle of restoration. Abraham was very old and Sarah was past the age of childbearing, but God restored her and made her fruitful.

In obedience to God, and faith in His promises, Abraham prepared to offer up Isaac as a sacrifice. In the mountains of Moriah, the same place where centuries later God's only begotten Son was to be crucified, Abraham and Isaac prefigured what God would do through Jesus.

Since God promised him many descendants through Isaac, Abraham believed that God would resurrect his son and for the three-day journey to the mountain Isaac was as good as dead in Abraham's mind. On the last stretch of the journey, father and son went on alone, up the mountain together, the son carrying the wood for the sacrifice on his back just as Jesus, Abraham's descendant and God's Son, would carry His Cross on that same mountain.

> *By faith Abraham, when he was tested, offered up Isaac, and he who had received the promises offered up his only begotten son, of whom it was said "In Isaac your seed shall be called," accounting that God was able to raise him up, even from the dead, from which he also received him in a figurative sense. (Hebrews 11:17–19)*

God stayed Abraham's hand and provided a ram as a substitute sacrifice. Abraham called the place *Jehovah Jireh*, meaning "The Lord Will Provide." From the sacrifice of a beloved Son by the Father, all the provision of God flows.

Abraham was called the Friend of God. God would call Abraham's descendants, the nation of Israel, His Son (Exodus 4:22). Abraham willingly offered his son to God, therefore God considered Isaac and all who came from him to be the Son of God. Isaac was a type of the One who was to come. God's Son, Jesus, would be Abraham's descendant (Galatians 3:16). All who are in Christ are Abraham's heirs (Galatians 3:29) and co-heirs with Christ of God (Romans 8:17). From this faith-filled human/divine relationship will come the restoration of the Earth. Man is called into partnership with Almighty God to bring it about.

Chapter 3. The Other Bible Code

The discovery of an equidistant letter sequence (ELS) code in the Torah (the first five books of the Bible) intrigued and excited many. Though its existence was suspected for a long time, the invention of high-speed computers helped to verify it. Many modern-day events were found encoded in the Bible. For some it confirmed what they already knew—that God is indeed all-wise and all-knowing. The skeptics, as usual, require more convincing.

There is another code in the Bible which—to those who apply the code—brings an astounding revelation of the wisdom and knowledge of God and which will lay to rest any doubts about the inspiration of the Scriptures. This code is a key which unlocks the deeper secrets of the Bible and brings levels of understanding beyond the surface story. It throws light on the past and the present and reveals the way ahead. This code shows that God's plan for the Church is not some rescue from Heaven out of the escalating chaos in the Earth but, rather, that the Church is destined for a great and glorious victory in the Earth which will usher in the Kingdom of God on Earth as it is in Heaven. The code which reveals all this is called "Typology."

The principle of typology is "First the Natural, then the Spiritual" (as in 1 Corinthians 15:46).

God demonstrates in the physical realm what He intends to do in the spiritual. These types are physical or natural demonstrations of spiritual things. They are:

"a shadow of things to come but the substance is of Christ" (Colossians 2:17)

"the copy and shadow of heavenly [or spiritual] *things"* (Hebrews 8:5)

"examples"—*tupos* or types (1 Corinthians 10:11)

The types all point to Jesus and through Him to the purpose and destiny of the Church. Jesus said, *"You search the Scriptures, for in them you think you have eternal life; and these are they which testify of Me"* (John 5:39).

The Scriptures to which He was referring were, of course, the Old Testament Scriptures. As He walked with two of His followers on the way to Emmaus after the Resurrection, Jesus opened the Scriptures to them: *"And beginning at Moses and all the Prophets, He expounded to them in all the Scriptures the things concerning Himself"* (Luke 24:27).

"Moses" is a reference to the first five books of the Bible which God inspired Moses to write. Jesus can be seen in every book of the Bible, not just in the surface prophecies but in the types and shadows which God has put there for those who will continue to "search the Scriptures." Under the direction of the Holy Spirit, truth continues to pour from the pages of God's Word and each truth reveals another flawless facet of the Son of God. This revelation of Christ in the Old Testament Scriptures is hidden from those who do not receive Him. As Paul states:

But their minds were hardened. For until this day the same veil remains unlifted in the reading of the Old Testament, because the veil is taken away in Christ. But even to this day, when

Moses is read, a veil lies on their heart. Nevertheless when one turns to the Lord, the veil is taken away. (2 Corinthians 3:14–16)

The Gospel is simple yet very profound. The Good News of God's love and forgiveness in Jesus Christ is such that anyone with an open heart can receive it. However, there are depths to be plumbed only by earnest seekers. God is careful where He casts His choicest pearls of truth. They are not for profane eyes, but for those who will value them and use them for His glory. When Jesus preached to the multitudes He spoke in parables—simple stories of everyday life—but as the disciples inquired of Him, He revealed the deeper truth of the parables *"as they were able to hear it"* (Mark 4:33).

The mysteries of the Kingdom of God are for those who will Ask, Seek, and Knock. They are closed to those who do not honour God's Word or who are not open to the ongoing revelation of the Spirit. Jesus said to the lawyers, the teachers of the day, *"...you have taken away the key of knowledge. You did not enter in yourselves, and those who were entering in you hindered"* (Luke 11:52).

The liberals of today with their watered-down version of the Bible cannot be custodians of the Key. Degrees and doctorates, though they may supply some useful tools such as an understanding of Greek and Hebrew, do not make a teacher of the truths of God. They are not acquired academically, but by revelation of the Word and the Spirit. Jesus said, *"I thank You, Father, Lord of heaven and earth, because You have hidden these things from the wise and prudent and have revealed them to babes"* (Matthew 11:25).

A Parable is an earthly story with a heavenly meaning. Similarly, a Type is a physical object or happening which demonstrates a spiritual truth and, as Watchman Nee truly said, Christ is the sum of all spiritual things. Out in the wilderness when God instructed Moses to strike the rock, He was telling us something about Christ; the brazen serpent on the pole and each piece of furniture in the Tabernacle were telling us something about Christ. God gave or did nothing capriciously; it all had meaning. Because the Spirit was available to only a select few in Old Testament days, truth was encoded in the types, ready to be revealed by the ongoing work of the Spirit, available to all believers after the Resurrection. Many precious truths are portrayed in Old Testament Scriptures which are neglected or practically discarded by some sections of the Church today, e.g., the Scriptures concerning the Tabernacle. These Scriptures are often thought of as irrelevant for today, but they hold the key to understanding where the Church is now on God's agenda and to what lies ahead.

Typology is open to misuse. There has been some weird and wonderful preaching which was purportedly based on typology. However, we are less likely to err if we stay with the central redemptive acts of God in the Old Testament. Since the Cross of Christ is the only means of redemption, all redemptive acts point to it. The three main types are:

· The Feasts of Israel,
· The Tabernacle or Temple, and
· The Journey to the Promised Land

The types provide windows through which we can view with far greater clarity the events of the New Testament. For example, Moses' smiting of the rock in Exodus 17 and again in Numbers 20 were not just historical happenings, but the enactment of spiritual truth which finds its fulfillment in the Cross of Christ, and which is applicable to us today.

The New is in the Old concealed; the Old is in the New revealed.
The New is in the Old enfolded; the Old is in the New unfolded.
The New is in the Old contained; the Old is in the New explained.

Israel, the Demonstration Nation

God demonstrates through the nation of Israel His will and purpose for the Church. His purposes are:

- *Demonstrated in Israel.* The pattern is set in God's redemptive acts in the nation. Into these patterns God encoded His strategy for bringing about the restoration of all things.
- *Fulfilled in Christ.* Made possible through the Cross and Resurrection. Through Jesus, the physical pattern becomes the spiritual reality.
- *Manifested through the Church.* Actualized by the Church laying hold of what the Cross has purchased.

Looking at the pattern in the types helps us to see what is ours to claim and how to claim it. If we can grasp that, then the whole Bible will open up in a new way.

Please note: this is not what is called "Replacement Theology" but, rather, Parallel Theology. Israel has a pivotal part to play in God's great plan of Restoration. His planned path for Israel and for the Church will merge and become one in these last days. One of the things that *Elijah* will do is turn the hearts of the fathers to the children and the hearts of the children to their fathers (Malachi 4:5). Judaism is the father of the Christian faith. There will be and is even now a coming together of the Old and New Covenant people of God in Christ Jesus. The number of Messianic Jews is rapidly increasing and ultimately *"...all Israel will be saved"* (Romans 11:20).

Abraham's physical descendants through Isaac are the nation of Israel; his spiritual descendants are all who are in Christ through faith, i.e., the Church. *"And if you are Christ's, then you are Abraham's seed and heirs according to the promise"* (Galatians 3:29). (References to "the Church" in this book are not about the institution of the Church or any denomination, but about all true believers in Christ.)

God's promises to Abraham concerning his descendants have a physical fulfillment in Israel and a spiritual fulfillment in the Church. Everything God does in and through Israel has a spiritual parallel in the Church. The destiny of the Church therefore, is inextricably linked with that of Israel. Our past, present, and future are written into the nation's history. Even now, as we see Israel under pressure, with enemies on every side who have openly stated their intent to eliminate them, we can see the spiritual battle in which the Church is engaged. The Israelis cannot afford to let their guard down for a minute; neither can we. For example, there was a time when, in Christian-based countries, we could take traditional Christian values for granted. Not anymore! Humanism, with its stated intent to remove belief in God from society, is constantly on the attack. Compromise or appeasement may seem to be the answer for Israel and for us, but they are not according to the will of God.

For the purpose of this book we will be concentrating mainly on the Journey to the Promised Land and touching on the Feasts and the Tabernacle. 1 Corinthians 10:1–11 tells us that the things that happened to the Israelites on the way to the Promised Land were our *"examples"* and *"written for our admonition, on whom the ends of the ages have come"* (1 Corinthians 10:11). The Greek word for "example" here is *tupos*, or "type."

Israel could not have known the full implication of the events of the journey, but the means of the restoration of all things is encrypted into them. God caused them to be written especially with us in mind.

The revelation by which the Church advances is a deeper understanding of the Cross. Speculation over the identity of the Antichrist or Gog and Magog, etc., occupies much of the thinking and preaching on end times these days. While this information may or may not be relevant and useful, our focus must always be on the answer—the Cross of Christ—not on the problems and the ploys of the enemy encountered along the way. The truth that will be our guiding light is the unfolding revelation of the Cross. Before He returned to Heaven, Jesus told His disciples:

"I still have many things to say to you, but you cannot bear them now, However, when He, the Spirit of truth, has come, He will guide you into all truth; for He will not speak on His own authority, but whatever He hears He will speak; and He will tell you things to come." (John 16:12, 13)

It was all too huge to be understood at once.

"Whom will he teach knowledge?

And whom will he make to understand the message?

Those just weaned from milk?

Those just drawn from the breasts?

For precept must be upon precept, precept upon precept,

Line upon line, line upon line,

Here a little, there a little." (Isaiah 28:9, 10)

Unfortunately, all too often Christians close their minds to any further revelation, and so cannot receive ongoing vision. We have not yet come into all truth and, now more than ever, we need light on things to come. One of the ways that the Holy Spirit teaches truth and shows things to come is by typology. It is, as previously stated, a code whereby spiritual truth is revealed through the physical events described in the Old Testament.

The future can be unlocked not by looking at the end of the Book (trying to interpret the book of Revelation) but by looking at the front of the Book—at God's dealings with the Demonstration Nation. The more revelation we have on the front of the Book, the more the mysteries of the book of Revelation will unfold. The code for deciphering God's plan for the future lies in His dealings with His people in the past.

> *The code for deciphering God's plan for the future lies in His dealings with His people in the past.*

Most Christians have understood that the Passover lamb—which secured the release of Israel from slavery in Egypt—foreshadowed Jesus, the Lamb of God, whose shed blood brings us out from the power of darkness and bondage to sin and death. Redemption through the blood of the Passover lamb is a clear type of our redemption through the sacrifice of *"The Lamb of God who takes away the sin of the world!"* (John 1:29). We need to follow the type through to its conclusion. When we do, we will be able to look back and see the way that God has brought us and also see clearly the way ahead. We will see, too, that not only did Jesus fulfill the types, but His life and ministry followed the pattern in the types. Biblical truth is always established by two or three witnesses (2 Corinthians 13:1). The pattern laid down in Israel was repeated in the life of Jesus and is the pattern for the Church. It is a guide we can trust. The first Passover in Egypt was the beginning of a journey.

Chapter 4. The Unfinished Journey

The most important journey in all of Earth's history is the one on which the Church is traveling. The completion of this journey will change the world forever. When Israel finished the journey, for a short while they became what God intended them to be: a light to the nations, a demonstration of the rule of the Kingdom. Jesus completed the journey and planted the Kingdom of God in the Earth. When the Church completes the journey, that Kingdom will come "on Earth as it is in Heaven" and Jesus will reign. The Earth will be an extension of Heaven, as it was created to be. The time is coming when *"the earth shall be full of the knowledge of the Lord"* (Isaiah 11:9). The promised new Earth (Revelation 21:1) is actually a renewed or refreshed Earth, not new in respect to age. The Spirit *"renew[s] the face of the Earth"* (Psalm 104:30). It is a *"restoration of all things"* (Acts 3:21; emphasis added).

Most Christians are aware that the Church is at a crucial time. We are on the verge of something big. Many frightening and bewildering things are happening on planet Earth. What's up ahead? Some think that it's not our problem because Jesus is coming very soon to snatch us out of the chaos; others aren't so sure. There's confusion in the camp. What is needed is a map that will show the way ahead.

Our code reveals that the Bible contains such a map. God Himself charted it with the Pillar of Cloud and Fire as He led His people to the Promised Land. It is a physical map of a spiritual journey. The map has been there under our noses all along. The problem is that we haven't recognized it for what it is. We thought it was all about Heaven and dying, e.g., *"When I tread the verge of Jordan, bid my anxious fears subside; death of death, and hell's destruction, land me safe on Canaan's side..."* ("Guide Me, O Thou Great Jehovah," *Australian Hymn Book*, song 478, by William Williams).

Is the Promised Land a type of Heaven? A land which has to be conquered? Giants? Strongholds? I don't think so! Our understanding of what the Promised Land represents is crucial. It holds the key to our destiny and thus directs our mission. Our vision for the future determines our actions now.

The experiences of Israel on the epic journey have inspired and challenged multitudes of Christians during their earthly pilgrimage, and rightly so. We are assured that there are better things ahead and that our faithful God will get us there.

All who die in the Lord will certainly be ushered into the portals of Heaven. Ultimately, however, the Promised Land is a land to be possessed by the people of God this side of Heaven. In fact, possession of the Promised Land will bring Heaven to Earth. How can we know that?

When Israel first came to the borders of the Land two years after coming out of Egypt, God told Moses to send twelve spies to spy it out. All of the spies agreed that it was a good land, but only two—Joshua and Caleb—thought that it could be conquered. The other ten thought that the giants and strongholds in the land made it impregnable. Israel refused to enter. Only the intercession of Moses saved them from being disinherited. God pardoned them but made a vow: *"but truly, as I live, all the earth shall be filled with the glory of the Lord"* (Numbers 14:21).

What does this statement, made at this particular point, mean but that the glory of the Lord filling the Earth is dependent on the people of God possessing the Promised Land?

When the glory of the Lord fills the Earth, that will be Heaven on Earth.

Israel refused to enter the Land, but a generation would arise which would fulfill the commission. Then the Glory of God would fill the Earth. Of the adults present in Israel at that time, only those who had exercised faith—Joshua and Caleb—ultimately made it into the Land. They persevered because they had a burning vision of what could be, and when they finally entered the Land thirty-eight years later, they had with them a multitude of new-generation warriors who were convinced that, under God, they could possess the Land...and they did!

Eventually Solomon, the son of David, came to the throne. A great golden temple was built and, at its dedication, the Glory of the Lord filled it. The nation was at its zenith, a light to the world. It was a faint, earthly picture of what our Earth will be like when the Greater Son of David, our Lord Jesus Christ, sits on the throne and the glory of the Lord fills the Earth.

That is dependent on the people of God possessing the Land. What is the Land? The Promised Land is the Earth—our lost inheritance, regained in Christ and yet to be possessed for the Kingdom. The Land was not like Heaven when Israel entered; it became like Heaven when they overcame the enemy and established the rule of God. The Promised Land possessed by the People of God, is the Kingdom of God on Earth as it is in Heaven. This is the goal toward which God has been working since Man fell and Eden was lost.

The cup of Elijah—the fifth cup with its great promise, "I will take you into the Land"—remains on the table at the Jewish Passover. It is still not drunk. Even though the Jews possessed the land of Canaan, even though they have been brought back into the Land after almost two thousand years of exile, they recognize that there is yet a far greater fulfillment of the promise. *Elijah* has yet to come and restore all things. The Golden Age lies ahead.

The cup of Elijah is filled from the cups of all present at the Passover feast. What does that mean? *Elijah* is made up of the Covenant people of God who together will come *"in the spirit and power of Elijah"* to restore all things; overthrow the powers of darkness; possess the Land; bring repentance and reconciliation; and turn the Earth back to God. *Elijah* will prepare the way of the Lord.

Chapter 5. The Code and the Great Commission

Jesus said,

> *"All authority has been given to Me in heaven and earth. Go therefore and make disciples of all the nations, baptizing them in the name of the Father and of the Son and of the Holy Spirit, teaching them to observe all things that I have commanded you; and lo, I am with you always, even to the end of the age."* *(Matthew 28:18–20)*

Before returning to the Father, Jesus commissioned the infant Church. He gave what seems to be a tall order. They were to make disciples of all the nations. Looking at the enormity of the Commission, it is easy to understand why the human mind balks and rationalizes it to mean, "Make some disciples from out of every nation." Make all the nations Jesus' disciples? How realistic is that? Most of the people of Israel were just as incredulous back in the Numbers incident (Numbers 13 and 14). "Conquer Canaan? Look at the giants and walled cities. Let's be realistic here!"

To possess the Promised Land and establish the Kingdom was the Great Commission of the Old Testament. How they eventually accomplished the task is the code which reveals how the Church will fulfill the Great Commission of the New Testament. "Realistic" or "unrealistic" aren't in God's vocabulary. What He has purposed is totally possible because He IS God. Humanly speaking, how "realistic" was the Resurrection? For *"...with God all things are possible"* (Matthew 19:26).

The Commission that Jesus gave the Church is a mandate to reclaim the Earth for God.

The Commission that Jesus gave the Church is a mandate to reclaim the Earth for God. To make disciples means to bring people under the rule of God. That's what the Kingdom is—the rule of God. To make disciples of all the nations is to establish the Kingdom of God on the Earth. This is the New Testament fulfillment of what the Old Testament people of God were called to do. Liberated from bondage in Egypt, armed at Mount Sinai with the Tabernacle and the Law and God's promise of victory, they were to conquer the enemy, possess the Land, and establish the rule of God, i.e., the Kingdom. They were called to be *"a kingdom of priests and a holy nation"* (Exodus 19:6). The dedication of the Temple by Solomon, son of David, was the climax of Israel's mission. At this great event, all the redemptive types of the Old Testament converge and are fulfilled. (See illustration.)

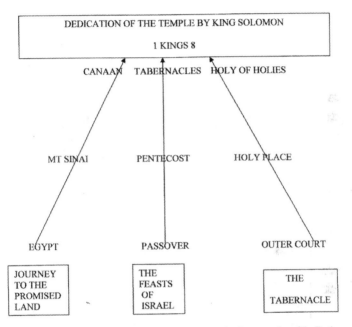

The three main Old Testament Types which project God's plan for the restoration of the Earth converge and climax in the great event of the dedication of the Temple by King Solomon. The Enemy had been subdued and the Land repossessed by the people of God. The Kingdom had been established and the Son of David was on the throne. The Glory of God filled the Temple. The final harvest was in and the Feast of Tabernacles — a time of great joy, was being celebrated.

This is a picture of what God has in store for the Earth. The effects of the Enemy's intrusion and influence in the Earth will be obliterated and the Earth renewed. Jesus, Son of David will rule, the harvest of souls will be complete and the Glory of God will fill the Earth.

"At this great event all the redemptive types of the Old Testament converge and are fulfilled"

As with all types, here the type breaks down. Solomon the king and the people of Israel went into spiritual decline and the time of peace and prosperity came to an end. Types are only shadows of the reality in Christ, which will be permanent. Nevertheless, the conquest of the Promised Land by a nation of former slaves is a clear pattern which God has set before us to show the destiny He has planned for the Church.

Jesus taught us to pray that God's Name be hallowed, His will be done, and His kingdom come on the Earth as it is in Heaven. If this were to happen automatically at some predetermined time, why would Jesus teach this prayer? Prayer is asking for things that will not happen unless we pray. The establishment of the Kingdom of God on Earth is the responsibility of the Church. Israel was not alone and neither are we. When they finally set themselves to be obedient, all the hosts of Heaven worked with them and the seemingly impossible mission was accomplished.

As He walked out of the temple in Jerusalem for the last time, Jesus said, *"See! Your house is left to you desolate; for I say to you, you shall see Me no more till you say 'Blessed is He who comes in the Name of the Lord!'"* (Matthew 23:38, 39). In other words, "You won't see Me again until you want Me." This was spoken primarily to Israel but also to the whole Earth. Jesus will come again when the people of the Earth cry out for His return.

The Kingdom of God on Earth as it is in Heaven, is God's answer to this hurting world. God created a beautiful world which reflected His Glory. The Earth was corrupted, and pain and suffering came into the world with the entry of sin. Adam transferred his allegiance from God to Satan and so handed his God-given dominion to the enemy. Satan is the *"prince of the power of the air, the spirit who now works in the sons of disobedience"* (Ephesians 2:2). He is *"the god of this age"* who has blinded the minds of those who are perishing (2 Corinthians 4:3, 4). He, with his minions, the principalities and powers and spiritual hosts of wickedness (Ephesians 6:12), hold most of the inhabitants of the Earth captive in chains of darkness.

Ephesians 4:17–19 describes the human condition outside of Christ:

...the Gentiles walk in the futility of their mind, having their understanding darkened, being alienated from the life of God, because of the ignorance that is in them, because of the hardening of their heart; who, being past feeling, have given themselves over to licentiousness, to work all uncleanness with greediness.

Does God still love them? Resoundingly, Yes! God still *so* loves the people of the world and doesn't want any to perish but all to come to repentance (2 Peter 3:9). God wants all people everywhere to come out of the darkness of Satan's domain and into His Kingdom of light and love. At the Cross, Jesus prayed, *"Father, forgive them, for they do not know what they do"* (Luke 23:34).

The people of the Earth outside of Christ are in spiritual blindness and still don't know what they're doing as they continue in a hopeless, lost state, that spirals downward into destruction, creating waves of havoc and pain. Jesus didn't call them "wicked," just "lost," and He came *"to save that which is lost"* (Matthew 18:11). *"For God did not send His Son into the world to condemn the world, but that the world through Him might be saved"* (John 3:17).

As we have seen, the Bible shows that Creation reflects the spiritual state of man, that's why *"...the creation eagerly waits for the revealing of the sons of God...because the creation itself also will be delivered from the bondage of corruption into the glorious liberty of the children of God"* (Romans 8:19, 21).

Our lost inheritance has been regained for us by Jesus. He has taken authority back from Satan and delegated it to us. However, Satan continues to exercise authority in the Earth by default. We are the rightful heirs, but our Promised Land is occupied by "giants" of wickedness and "strongholds" of evil, and has to be conquered.

Let's take a little foray into this land we are called to possess. You can do it from the comfort of your recliner chair in front of the TV or by reading a newspaper or magazine. What do you see? Some good things, yes! But also a world in which there is much turmoil and entrenched hatred and rebellion against God—riots, terrorism, greed, corruption, violence, pornography, the escalation of false religion, and persecution of godly people; and worldliness, compromise, and unbelief in much of the organization of the Church—giants and strongholds galore.

We are faced with enormous obstacles that to the human mind seem insurmountable. Can we conquer the Land for God? Ten of the spies that Moses sent into the Land looked at the obstacles that confronted them and said, "No way." Joshua and Caleb looked at God and said, *"they are our bread"* (Numbers 14:9). In other words, "We'll eat them."

Why was Moses told to send out the spies? God already knew what the Land was like. Israel needed to see it for themselves, to be aware of all the facts but then to believe that God was bigger than it all—that the redemption He had brought to them made them more than conquerors. It was a faith test and He was after a faith confession. Without faith they would fail miserably. Caleb and Joshua saw the obstacles too, but they put God into the equation. They said, *"Let us go up at once and take possession, for we are well able to overcome it"* (Numbers 13:30).

"If the Lord delights in us, then He will bring us into the land and give it to us, 'a land which flows with milk and honey.' Only

do not rebel against the LORD, nor fear the people of the land, for they are our bread; <u>their protection has departed from them, and the LORD is with us</u>. Do not fear them." (Numbers 14:8, 9; emphasis added)

Thirty-eight years later, Joshua and Caleb made it in. The rest of that generation (those over the age of twenty) perished in the wilderness.

If the Earth is indeed the Land we are called to possess, where do you stand? With Joshua and Caleb, or with the rest? Can we possess it for God? Your answer will depend on your understanding of the greatness of His provision in the Cross of Christ. There are any number of people who, like the ten spies, are ready to give a bad report. We hear a lot about how things are going from bad to worse, and so they are. There are not a lot of Christians saying that we can take the world for God. Joshua and Caleb saw the giants and the strongholds too, but they looked beyond that to the spiritual realities. They saw that God was for them and that the enemy was a defeated foe. When God brought the nation to the borders of the Land the second time, He took them by a different route and gave them a deeper revelation of their deliverance. This is what we need before the Church is ready to conquer and possess the Land.

In order to come into that deeper revelation we need to retrace the journey from the beginning, keeping in mind the principle of the code, "First the Natural, then the Spiritual" or "Demonstrated in Israel; Fulfilled in Christ; Manifested through the Church." This will bring the record of an ancient journey into a present and powerful reality. We will build *"precept upon precept and line upon line"* and, hopefully, by the end of the journey we will have all climbed Faith Mountain and surveyed the 360° view. You will need a conviction that the Bible is the Word of God, one pair of Holy Spirit binoculars, and a mind that is open to new revelation.

Paul prays for us:

[For I always pray] the God of our Lord Jesus Christ, the Father of Glory, that He may grant you a spirit of wisdom and revelation – of insight into mysteries and secrets—in the [deep and intimate] knowledge of Him,

By having the eyes of your heart flooded with light, so that you can know and understand the hope to which He has called you and how rich is His glorious inheritance in the saints—His set-apart ones,

And [so that you can know and understand] what is the immeasurable and unlimited and surpassing greatness of His power in and for us who believe, as demonstrated in the working of His mighty strength,

Which He exerted in Christ when He raised Him from the dead and seated Him at His [own] right hand in the heavenly [places],

Far above all rule and authority and power and dominion, and every name that is named—above every title that can be conferred—not only in this age and in this world, but also in the age and the world which are to come. (Ephesians 1:17–21, The Amplified Bible)

We will trace the Journey of Israel and see the parallel in the life of Christ and the life of the believer, and also in the history of the Church. Since the events of the Journey were marked by special days or Feasts in Israel, we will look briefly at the relation of the Feasts to the Journey; we will also briefly consider the Tabernacle. The Journey is divided into three main parts: the Escape from Egypt, the Equipping of the People of God, and the Conquest of Canaan.

The Escape from Egypt is about how God brings His people out from under the power of the kingdom of darkness ruled by *"the god of this age"* (2 Corinthians 4:4).

The Conquest of Canaan shows how the people of God will overthrow the evil one and establish the rule of God in the Earth.

The part of the Journey in between is where God equips His people for the task ahead, changing a rabble of slaves into an army of Overcomers. It is a journey of faith where we learn to operate out of our new identity in Christ. (See illustration.)

"a physical map of a spiritual journey"

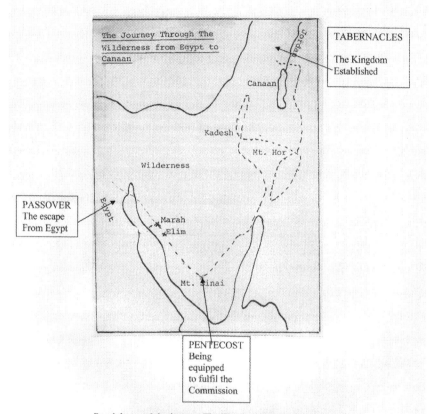

Regaining our Inheritance – The Kingdom of God on Earth

Lost in Adam – Regained in Christ

"For the promise that he would be heir of the world (was) not to Abraham or to his seed through the law, but through the righteousness of faith. Romans 4:13

"And if you are Christ's then you are Abraham's seed, and heirs according to the promise."
Galatians 3:29

Chapter 6. The Code in the Escape from Egypt

Over 400 years have elapsed since Father Abraham was called out of Ur to become the Friend of God and His representative in the Earth. Through him, God would begin the work of restoration. God had made many promises to him concerning his Seed; however, the descendants of Abraham, far from being a blessing to the Earth, are in slavery in the land of Egypt, which is ruled by a merciless tyrant.

Three generations have passed. The glowing promises of blessing, peace, prosperity, and an eternal inheritance, if remembered at all, seem like some faint, impossible dream. The present is painful and the future seems to hold little hope. Their promised inheritance is under the control of a depraved and polluted people. (Scriptures such as Genesis 6:4 and Numbers 13:32, 33 seem to indicate that they were a hybrid race, the result of their intermingling with the fallen angels.)

Israel is the nation which God calls "My Son" (Exodus 4:22). Why has God allowed His Son to come to this pitiful state of affairs? Before Isaac was even born God told Abraham that it would be so:

"Know certainly that your descendants will be strangers in a land that is not theirs, and will serve them, and they will afflict them 400 years.

And also the nation whom they serve, I will judge; afterward they shall come out with great possessions...But in the fourth generation they shall return here..." (Genesis 15:13–16)

Abraham experienced something of the *"horror and great darkness"* which would befall his descendants (Genesis 15:12). But God made a Blood Covenant with him and swore that the Land of Promise would belong to his Seed (Genesis 15:18–21).

Israel, as we have said, is the Demonstration Nation. While being the people through whom God would bring blessing to the world, they were also to be an example of the sinful state of mankind. In this way, they would portray the state of fallen humanity and God's miraculous deliverance. This darkness would descend upon the Greater Son, Jesus, when He was on the Cross bearing the sins of the world.

The state of fallen Mankind was of *"having no hope and without God in the world"* (Ephesians 2:12), *"slaves of sin"* (Romans 6:17), and under condemnation and death. As Israel was in a land *"that is not theirs,"* so fallen humanity was also dwelling in a land which was not theirs: an Earth ruled by Satan, *"the ruler of this world"* (John 12:31) more merciless than the Pharaoh of old, assisted by demonic hordes, *"spiritual hosts of wickedness in the heavenly places"* (Ephesians 6:13). However, the Blood Covenant that God made with Abraham was also made with his Seed. Into this seemingly hopeless situation deliverance was to come.

The predicted 400 years of bondage was drawing to a close when God raised up a deliverer—Moses, chosen to lead the people out of Egypt and into the Promised Land. His birth was accompanied by the slaughter of innocent infants, as was that of Jesus, the Redeemer Who was to come. Moses was brought up in the palace but choose *"to suffer affliction with the people of God"* (Hebrews 11:25). Jesus came *"out of the ivory palaces"* (Psalm 45:8) and made the descent into our suffering humanity. Under God's chosen deliverer redemption and, ultimately, restoration was on the way.

Moses was sent to tell Pharaoh that God required the release of Israel:

> *Then you shall say to Pharaoh, "Thus says the Lord: 'Israel is My son, My firstborn. So I say to you, let My son go that he may serve Me. But if you refuse to let him go, indeed I will kill your son, your firstborn.'" (Exodus 4:22, 23)*

To move Pharaoh to comply, God sent a series of plagues. Israel was kept safe and unaffected by them. The final plague was the slaying of the firstborn. The people of Israel were told to mark their doors with the blood of a lamb. God said, *"And when I see the blood, I will pass over you; and the plague shall not be on you to destroy you when I strike the land of Egypt"* (Exodus 12:13).

The blood put a dividing line between the redeemed and the condemned. Placing the blood on the door was an act of faith. It saved the occupants from judgment and put them on God's side of the dividing line. The Feast of Passover was established as a memorial to this great deliverance (Exodus 12).

God told them that this was to be a new beginning for the nation of Israel, a "beginning of months." All the congregation of Israel was to choose a lamb on the tenth day of the month, a male in its prime. It was kept for four days and examined for blemishes. Only a perfect lamb could be offered. The lamb had to be killed at twilight (literally between the two evenings), roasted in fire, and eaten. No bone was to be broken. (Note: The Jews had two evenings. The first was 3:00 p.m. at which time the evening sacrifice was killed; the second was at 6:00 p.m. or near sunset.)

Christ, Our Passover

As Jesus rode into Jerusalem on that first Palm Sunday many centuries later, the crowds acclaimed Him as a king. Little did they realize that they were choosing their Passover lamb, a Lamb for the nation and ultimately for the whole world. Jerusalem was the only place where sacrifice could be made, and Israel, as the priestly nation, was the only nation which could make the sacrifice.

The Passover Lamb had to be perfect with no blemishes. Over the next few days, Jesus presented Himself in the Temple where He was examined by the scribes, the Pharisees, and the Sadducees who tried to trick Him in His words, to no avail. After His arrest He was examined by every authority in Jerusalem: Pilate the governor, the Chief Priest, and King Herod. Finally, Pilate pronounced, "I find no fault in Him." The Lamb was pronounced perfect; *"knowing that you were not redeemed with corruptible things, like silver or gold...but with the precious blood of Christ, as of a lamb without blemish and without spot"* (1 Peter 1:18, 19).

Jesus died at 3:00 p.m., the time of the evening sacrifice. He fulfilled the type of the Passover lamb perfectly, even to the instruction that no bone was to be broken. As He hung on the Cross, He stood between sinful humanity and the wrath (fire) of God against sin.

When we by faith apply the blood of Jesus to our lives we have our personal Passover. We are justified by faith in the blood of the Lamb. *"Therefore, being justified by faith, we have peace with God through our Lord Jesus Christ"* (Romans 5:1). Justification deals with the penalty for sin. We are not under condemnation anymore.

After the slaying of the firstborn, while it was yet dark, Pharaoh urged Israel to leave. They set out toward the Red Sea, pausing at Succoth to bake cakes from the dough they had brought from Egypt which was unleavened because of their haste. Before them went the Presence of God, manifested in a Pillar of Cloud by day and Fire by night. Through their entire journey, even in times of rebellion, the

Cloud went with them—leading them, protecting them, and providing shade by day and warmth and light by night.

In our spiritual pilgrimage, we have the assurance of God's Presence with us always. Though, like Israel, we often complain, rebel, and disbelieve, He remains faithful. Our strength and our peace lie not in our own wavering commitment to Him, but in the knowledge of His faithfulness to us.

"For He Himself has said, 'I will never leave you nor forsake you.'" (Hebrews 13:5)

"...lo, I am with you always, even to the end of the age." (Matthew 28:20)

God then sanctified them, i.e., He declared them holy, set apart for Himself. The firstborn of Israel were to be dedicated to the Lord (Exodus 13). Later the Lord took the tribe of Levi in place of the firstborn to serve Him in the Tabernacle. The <u>Feast of Unleavened Bread</u> marked this separation to God, leaven being a type of sin. Sanctification deals with the power of sin.

Jesus fulfilled this type by taking our sins upon Himself and burying them in His grave: *"who Himself bore our sins in His own body on the tree that we, having died to sins, might live for righteousness..."* (1 Peter 2:24).

His body went into the grave as the Feast of Unleavened Bread began. In Jesus, God declares us holy. We are *"sanctified in Christ Jesus called to be saints"* (1 Corinthians 1:2).

"But of Him you are in Christ Jesus, who became for us wisdom from God—and righteousness and sanctification and redemption" (1 Corinthians 1:30). Sin, and therefore Satan, no longer has dominion over us. We belong to God—His Own special people.

God sealed Israel's deliverance by the miracle of dividing the waters of the Red Sea as Pharaoh's armies followed them in hot pursuit. This was Israel's baptismal day. They were *"all baptized into Moses in the cloud and in the sea"* (1 Corinthians 10:2). Israel was first *"baptized in the cloud,"* that is, they were separated from their enemies by the action of the Pillar as it lifted and stood between them and Pharaoh's armies (Exodus 14:19, 20). Here we see in type the action of the Holy Spirit as He separates the believer from *"the power of darkness"* (Colossians 1:13) and immerses him into Christ. We are baptized by the Spirit into the Body of Christ. This is true of every believer. Then Israel was *"baptized in the sea."* The waters parted until Israel was safe on the other side, and then closed, burying their enemies beneath the waves. They were free from Egypt forever. Baptism is a sanctifying act. In water baptism we declare that we identify with Christ's death and resurrection and are dead to the world but alive to God.

Very early in the morning on the Sunday after the Crucifixion, a little band of priests would have made their way out of Jerusalem into the fields to reap a sheaf. This was then taken into the temple and waved before the Lord. It was the dedication of the first sheaf of the barley harvest, sometimes called the <u>Feast of Firstfruits</u> as commanded in Leviticus 23:10, 14. No one could partake of the harvest before this sheaf was dedicated.

At the same time the most momentous event in history was taking place. Christ rose from the dead, shattering the power of the enemy forever. No longer could the people of God be held captive. This was the promise of a great harvest to come—the Ransomed of all ages. *"But now Christ is risen from the dead, and has become the firstfruits of those who have fallen asleep"* (1 Corinthians 15:20).

Israel was the Firstfruits of the nations, the first sheaf of the harvest of nations. They were redeemed through the blood of the Passover lamb. *"Israel was holiness to the LORD, the firstfruits of His increase"* (Jeremiah 2:3).

Jesus' death, burial, and resurrection are foreshadowed in these three Feasts—Passover, Unleavened Bread, and Firstfruits—which together constitute the Festival of Passover. (See Leviticus 23:4–14.) The Feasts of Israel were memorials to a past event and prophetic of things to come.

Israel was *"baptized into Moses"* (1 Corinthians 10:2). We are baptized into Christ. Like Israel, we are set free to serve God. We come under the headship of Christ and share His life. *"But you are a chosen generation, a royal priesthood, a holy nation, His own special people, that you may proclaim the praises of Him who called you out of darkness into His marvelous light"* (1 Peter 2:9, cf. Exodus 19:5–7).

This Scripture is true of both Israel and the Church. The end purpose of the Church is, as it was for Israel, that God will have a special people through whom He can demonstrate the Kingdom and establish it. Christians are citizens of two kingdoms. They are in the world but not of the world. We are to live in this world by the principles of the Kingdom of God so that, through the Church, God can display the light of His holiness and love for all people and expand His Kingdom on the Earth.

On the Journey toward the Promised Land we learn to live by the principles of the Kingdom of God and not of the world—by faith and not by sight—just as Israel had to leave their slave mentality behind and learn to live as the people of God before they were ready to take possession of the Land. God's people are separated to Him, not so we can have a "holier-than-thou" attitude as the Pharisees did in Jesus' day, but to serve the world. As John 3:17 states, *"For God did not send His Son into the world to condemn the world, but that the world through Him might be saved."* We are not here to condemn the world but to be channels through which the world is saved. We will not serve the world or save the world by compromise with the world, but by demonstration of the Kingdom.

Our deliverance in Jesus is a spiritual parallel of the great deliverance of Israel from Egypt. They celebrated their victory on the shores of the Red Sea in dance and song. However, it was not the end of the journey, only the beginning. As Moses recounted later, *"...He brought us out from there, that He might bring us in, to give us the land of which He swore to our fathers"* (Deuteronomy 6:23). They were brought out in order to be brought in and possess the Land. The Church has yet to complete the Journey.

Chapter 7. The Code in Lessons Along the Way

The Eleven-Day Error

From time to time we hear some preacher say that it should have taken Israel only eleven days to reach the Promised Land but instead it was forty years. It was an eleven-day journey from Mount Sinai to Canaan (Deuteronomy 2:2) but God's timetable, from Egypt to the border of Canaan, was two years. There was some vital preparation to be done before they would be ready to possess the Land.

When God commissioned Moses at the foot of Mount Sinai, He told him it would be a sign that after the people had been brought out of Egypt, they would serve Him on that Mount. There was an important work to be done on Mount Sinai and lessons to be learned along the way. This rabble of ex-slaves had to become a mighty army and be equipped to be *"a kingdom of priests and a holy nation"* (Exodus 19:6).

Exodus 13:17, 18 tells us *"...God did not lead them by way of the Philistines, although that was near; for God said, 'Lest the people change their minds when they see war, and return to Egypt.' So God led the people around by way of the wilderness of the Red Sea."*

War was inevitable, but the people were not yet ready for it. Instead of heading northeast, towards Canaan, the Pillar of Cloud and Fire turned south and led the people toward Mount Sinai. The sojourn at Mount Sinai was an essential part of God's plan. This was Israel's Pentecost. There God came down in fire and wind and gave His redeemed people what they needed, to do the task to which He called them. At Mount Sinai He gave Israel the Law and the Tabernacle without which they could not have become *"a kingdom of priests, a holy nation."* Also, if they were to conquer the Promised Land, they had to come into the full realization that they were conquerors—that God was with them and they could do whatever He required of them. God had called them His Son (Exodus 4:22) and as God's Son, they were to execute God's will. Armed with truth, they would conquer.

The Wells of Marah and Elim—The
Healing Tree (Exodus 15:22–27)

After three days' journey into the Wilderness of Shur, the people thirsted. The Cloud led them to the waters of Marah. Here surely was relief at last. However, the waters of Marah were found to be bitter and undrinkable. (*Marah* in Hebrew means bitter.)

The exhilaration and joy of the Great Escape soon turned to disappointment and anger and the people complained to Moses; but an important lesson had to be demonstrated there and recorded for us *"upon whom the ends of the ages have come"* (1 Corinthians 10:11).

Following the Lord does not guarantee that there will not be bitter situations that confront us. We can complain or we can trust. We are on a pilgrimage and have not yet arrived at the blessedness of no more crying, pain, sorrow, or death that God has promised. Our comfort and our peace lie in trusting the One Who has left the Ivory Palaces and Halls of Glory to walk with us. God is faithful and is more than adequate in any situation.

God showed Moses a tree which, when cast into the bitter water, made it sweet and refreshed them. It was a healing tree, and there God revealed Himself as *Jehovah Rapha*—the Lord Who Heals. There is a Tree which, when applied to the bitterness and sorrow which the world experiences, will make all the difference. That Tree is the Cross of Christ. This Tree has the capacity to bring healing to the whole world. It heals our broken relationship with God and with each other. It will ultimately heal this whole sin-sick Creation. In the Cross of Christ, our spirit is healed when we are joined to God in the new birth; our soul or personality is being healed as we walk with God and apply His Word; and we can claim healing for our bodies. God has made provision for the healing of the whole person—spirit, soul, and body. Jesus went about healing all the sick who came to Him in faith, *"that it might be fulfilled which was spoken by Isaiah the prophet, saying: 'He Himself took our infirmities and bore our sicknesses'"* (Matthew 8:16, 17).

We see God's perfect will for Man displayed in Eden—wholeness of spirit, soul, and body. Disease came with the Fall.

The place of bitterness became the place of healing because of the healing Tree. When we are faced with adversity and are tempted to complain we can remember Marah. Marah was not a mistake on God's part; Marah became a miracle.

God has chosen us to be conformed to the likeness of Jesus. The Cross, for Jesus, meant taking the form of a servant and being obedient unto death. Taking up our Cross daily can mean being willing to be a servant to our fellow man and walking humbly with God through difficult circumstances. The Cross becomes a way of life. If we apply the Cross to the bitter situations that we encounter in our pilgrimage, they can become sweet as we experience *"the fellowship of His sufferings, being conformed to His death"* (Philippians 3:10).

A short way down the track *"they came to Elim where there were twelve wells of water and seventy palm trees"* (Exodus 15:27); there the people camped. Along the way our Guide ensures that there are times of rest and refreshing for His people.

Manna—Fed with Bread from Heaven (Exodus 16:1–21)

As they continued their journey through the Wilderness of Sin, the people were hungry and began to crave the food they had left behind in Egypt. They began to regret having undertaken the journey at all. There were some things about the life they had left that they sorely missed. The fact that they had been slaves and had been set free and made inheritors of the Land of Promise didn't seem to matter much by then. The fleshpots of Egypt loomed large in their memory. When we decide to follow Jesus, the indulgences of the past often beckon us back to the thinking and habits of the old life. The tempter is ever ready to lure us back to the old ways.

God provided quails for meat on this first occasion, and thereafter a daily provision of manna—bread from heaven. Manna is a type of the Word of God. Moses, recounting the journey as the Nation prepared to enter the Land, stated the purpose of the wilderness:

> *"And you shall remember that the Lord your God led you all the way these forty years in the wilderness, to humble you and test you, to know what was in your heart, whether you would keep His commandments or not.*
>
> *So He humbled you, allowed you to hunger, and fed you with manna which you did not know nor did your fathers know, that He might make you to know that man shall not live by bread alone; but man lives by every word that proceeds from the mouth of the Lord." (Deuteronomy 8:2, 3)*

Manna, which they or their fathers did not know, speaks of revelation through the Word. God had called them into a whole new life and that called for a new way of thinking and acting. Bread may sustain our bodies, but the Heavenly Manna sustains our souls and spirits. We progress in our pilgrimage by an ongoing revelation of the Word of God and our obedience to that Word. Daily the Spirit teaches us and renews our minds as we read God's Word. We are learning to think and act as Children of God: as Overcomers, not as slaves. The old ways of the world will have a diminishing influence on us as we take in the wonders of the Word.

Jesus said that He is the true Bread from Heaven. He is the Bread of Life. Jesus is the Living Word, which the written Word reveals. We celebrate this in Communion as we remember Jesus' words: *"Take, eat: this is My Body which is broken for you"* (1 Corinthians 11:24).

The new life in the Spirit is initiated and nurtured by the Living and written Word of God. That is why the enemy is always out to discredit, pollute, or compromise the Word. We are little threat to him and no help to the world if we disbelieve and disobey God's Word. Man brought disaster upon the world by not believing God's Word; we bring restoration by believing it.

The manna was to be collected and eaten daily except on the sixth day when they gathered enough for the Sabbath. Manna which was kept *"bred worms and stank"* (Exodus 16:20). This speaks of the necessity of an ongoing revelation of the Word. A Church that continually feeds on yesterday's manna will not progress into the purposes of God. It will become stale and lifeless.

The manna ceased when they entered the Land. A time will come when we will enter into the fullness of the revelation of Christ. Then we will be ready to overcome the enemy and possess the Land. Meanwhile we need to continue to feed on fresh manna.

Jesus, when He was tempted in the wilderness, chose to believe and obey the Word. He answered each temptation with "It is written…" and came out of the wilderness *"in the power of the Spirit"* and began to demolish the strongholds of the enemy (Luke 14:4). More on this later.

The Sabbath Rest—A Picture of Grace (Exodus 16:22–36)

On the sixth day Israel was to gather a double portion of manna to last through the Sabbath. Thus God impressed on them the importance of the Sabbath Rest. A "rest" in Scripture denotes a finished work. God brought Creation into being over six days and rested on the seventh, i.e., His work was finished. Adam and Eve opened their eyes on a perfect Creation. There was nothing they could do to add to it. Everything had been provided and they had only to rest in it, appreciate it, and care for it.

The Sabbath Day was a commemoration of God's finished work of Creation. When God gave the Commandments on Mount Sinai, a command to observe the Sabbath Rest was included. The Sabbath was kept to remember that there was a time when God finished His work of Creation. However, there remained a work for God to do. When the Jews criticized Jesus for healing on the Sabbath, He told them, *"My Father has been working until now, and I have been working."* (John 5:17). To the disciples He said, *"My food is to do the will of Him who sent Me, and to finish His work"* (John 4:34; emphasis added).

Sabbath-keeping is still a subject of debate among Christians. Saturday, the seventh day, was the Sabbath and still is for the Jews. Most Christians worship on Sunday in celebration of the Resurrection. Justyn Martyr, born about 100 AD, wrote:

And on the day called Sunday, all who live in cities or in the country gather together to one place, and the memoirs of the apostles or the writing of the prophets are read....Sunday is the day on which we hold our common assembly, because it is the first day on which God, having wrought a change in the darkness and matter, made the world; and Jesus Christ our Saviour on the same day rose from the dead. (The Ante-Nicene Fathers, Volume 1)

There are some who adhere to keeping Saturday as a Sabbath. Paul, in writing to the Church in Rome which included Jewish and Gentile believers, states that this should not be a cause for division among Christians. They were not to judge one another on this matter; Paul wrote, *"Let each be fully convinced in his own mind"* (Romans 14:5).

In Colossians 2:16, 17 Paul states that Christ fulfilled all the Holy Days of the Old Testament. They were "shadows" but the reality is Christ. The true Sabbath is a Person, not a day. Remembering the principle of the code "First the Natural then the Spiritual," the physical rest of the Old Covenant becomes the spiritual rest of Faith in the New Covenant. We rest in His finished work of Redemption, which is the New Creation.

The writer of Hebrews, in chapter 10:10–14, contrasts the work of the priests of the Old Covenant and the work of Jesus the Mediator of the New Covenant. The Old Covenant priests are pictured standing because their work was never finished. Sacrifices had to be continually made because they could not take away sin; they could only provide a covering for it until the one true sacrifice was made. In contrast, Jesus is seen seated at the right hand of the Father, waiting for His enemies to be made His footstool. Having made the one perfect sacrifice for all time, He is resting because His work is finished. In the matter of our Redemption, nothing remains to be done. By faith we rest in His finished work and through faith we release the benefits of that work into the Earth. This is an important truth and one which we will investigate further. Ultimately the whole Creation will celebrate an Eternal Sabbath Rest.

The Sabbath Rests of the Old Covenant were given to teach faith in God's finished work. His work is <u>His</u> work alone. The Great Day of Atonement was kept as a Sabbath. Everyone was forbidden to work because only the High Priest could make Atonement. Jesus is our Great High Priest and only He could do the work of Atonement. It is a perfect work and to think that we can add to it is presumption.

God's work is finished, therefore we can rest. The Sabbath Rest is a picture of Grace.

The Israelites, resting in their tents out in the wilderness, would not have understood all this. Again, it is recorded for our benefit as a code to be deciphered with the aid of the Holy Spirit.

What do we mean when we talk about the finished work of Christ? It means [as stated earlier] that everything that God is ever going to do in restoring the Earth has already been accomplished in seed form at the Cross. If it didn't happen at the Cross then it's never going to happen. Jesus has paid the full price for the reconciliation of all things to God (Colossians 1:19,20). All salvation, all healing, all reconciliation, all restoration has been purchased *"through the blood of His cross."* It is the faith of the Church which brings it into manifestation. Jesus prayed *"I have glorified You on the earth. I have finished the work which You have given Me to do"* (John 17:4). This is a vital end time truth which will empower us to possess the Land and a truth which I trust we will understand more fully by the end of this book. Anything less than total victory for the Church in the Earth falls short of the price paid at Calvary.

Anything less than total victory for the Church in the Earth falls short of the price paid at Calvary

---

Water from the Rock—The Cross Provides the
Life-Giving Spirit (Exodus 17:1–7)

Israel camped at Rephidim and there was no water to drink. Again the people complained and murmured against Moses. God told him to take his rod and strike a certain rock in Horeb on which He would stand and the rock would provide water. Moses did so and the people drank. This was more than a miracle of providing water to a thirsty people. In this incident God again encoded deep spiritual truths for us to decipher.

The Rock was a type of Christ. They *"...drank of that spiritual Rock that followed them, and that Rock was Christ"* (1 Corinthians 10:4; emphasis added).

God Himself would be standing on the Rock. Though the people could not see Him, God told Moses that He would be there. Moses was God's representative and the Rod was called the "Rod of God" (Exodus 17:9). God, through Moses, delivered the blow and God Himself took the blow. *"...God was in Christ reconciling the world to Himself,"* (2 Corinthians 5:19).

This is a picture of what God would do at the Cross. Moses represented God the Law-Giver. At Mount Sinai God would give the Law to Israel through Moses the Mediator. We have all broken God's Law and are therefore under judgment. God is a just God and must punish sin, but Jesus took upon Himself the sin of the whole world. As Isaiah predicted:

> *Surely He has borne our griefs and carried our sorrows;*
>
> *Yet we esteemed Him stricken, Smitten by God and afflicted.*
>
> *But He was wounded for our transgressions, He was bruised for our iniquities;*

The chastisement of our peace was upon Him, And by His stripes we are healed.

All we like sheep have gone astray; We have turned, every one, to his own way;

And the Lord has laid on Him the iniquity of us all. (Isaiah 53:4–6; emphasis added)

For He was cut off from the land of the living;

For the transgressions of My people He was stricken. (Isaiah 53:8)

The smitten Rock provided water for the thirsty people. Water is a type of the Spirit of God which Man lost at the Fall. We were separated from God, spiritually dead, *"dead in trespasses and sins"* (Ephesians 2:1). Through the crucified Christ—the smitten Rock—the demands of the Law were satisfied and God restored to us the life-giving Spirit.

In John 7:37–39 we read:

On the last day, that great day of the feast, Jesus stood and cried out, saying,

"If anyone thirsts, let him come to Me and drink.

He who believes in Me, as the Scripture has said,

out of his heart will flow rivers of living water."

But this He spoke concerning the Spirit, whom those believing in Him would receive;

for the Holy Spirit was not yet given, because Jesus was not yet glorified.

Later on in the Journey Moses was to strike the Rock again, but in doing so disqualified himself from entering the Land. This incident again provides clues to a vital truth, one which will empower us *"on whom the ends of the ages have come"* to enter and possess the Land.

Victory over Amelek—Prevailing Prayer in
the Name of Jesus (Exodus 17:8–16)

The enemy in Israel's history came in various guises: the Egyptians, the Amalekites, and the Canaanites, etc. All of these opposing forces are types of the one enemy: Satan, who opposes the will and purposes of God. Israel's battles portray the Church's ongoing struggle with that enemy.

At Rephidim the Amalekites attacked Israel. Moses instructed Joshua to lead the battle for Israel while he ascended an overlooking hill with Aaron and Hur. In his hands was the Rod of God. At the burning bush on Sinai, God had called Moses and commissioned him to deliver his people from Egypt. In answer to Moses' protestations of inadequacy, God said, *"What is that in your hand?"* (Exodus 4:2). In Moses' hand was a simple shepherd's rod, which he used to guide and protect the sheep. He was to use it many times as he shepherded Israel toward the Promised Land. God told him, *"And you shall take this rod in your hand, with which you shall do the signs"* (Exodus 4:17).

A rod is a symbol of authority. The scepter which the Queen holds is a symbol of her authority. Psalm 2 says that God's Anointed will rule the nations with a rod of iron.

The shepherd's rod became the Rod of God, and with it Moses exercised divine authority. With the Rod of God he brought plagues upon Egypt, parted the Red Sea, and brought water out of the Rock. The Rod of God got things done! Sometimes Aaron, as Moses' representative, used the Rod but it was "this Rod" by which the signs were done. Cast before Pharaoh, it became a serpent. When Pharaoh's magicians imitated this sign, the Rod of God devoured their rods—all earthly authority must yield to God's authority.

Now, as he stood on the hill overlooking the battlefield, Moses lifted up his hands in prayer with the Rod of God held high. So long as his hands were up, Israel prevailed; but when they came down, the battle turned. When he grew tired, Aaron and Hur sat Moses on a large stone and supported his hands. Eventually the battle was won.

Moses called the place *Jehovah Nissi*—meaning "the Lord is my banner"—for he said, *"...the Lord will have war with Amalek from generation to generation"* (Exodus 17:18). This would be an ongoing battle which every generation would have to undertake. A banner was a rod-like standard which, when held up, rallied an army to battle. At Rephidim that day there were more than human forces doing battle. The Rod of God brought hosts of Heaven into the fray, and Israel prevailed.

The Rod of God for us is the name of Jesus. At that name every knee must bow. In that name we have authority. Like Moses we may feel inadequate but we have the powerful name of Jesus to use. When a law officer exercises his duty "in the name of the law," all the weight of the law stands behind him. In the same manner, the name of Jesus carries the weight of His authority. Jesus was manifested to destroy the works of the devil (1 John 3:8). In His name we can enforce His victory. He said, *"Behold, I give you the authority to trample on serpents and scorpions, and over all the power of the enemy, and nothing shall by any means hurt you"* (Luke 10:19).

> ### The Rod of God for us is the name of Jesus

In His name the disciples of Jesus preached the Gospel, healed the sick, raised the dead, and cast out demons. Jesus gave us His name to use in prayer. He said, *"...whatever you ask the Father in My Name He will give you"* (John 16:23).

It is not just speaking the name of Jesus but understanding all that it represents that brings results. Holding up the Rod of God in prayer brings victory, and using the Rod against the works of the devil brings deliverance. With the Rod of God, the dominion which Adam lost is restored to God's people. All authority in heaven and earth has been given to Jesus and He has delegated that authority to us to use in His name. The principle of delegation is reinforced in the next incident.

Shepherding the People of God (Exodus 18)

Jethro, Moses' father-in-law, stood watching him as the people brought their concerns to him for counsel. Moses had shepherded the flocks of Jethro for many years. Now he had the care of the flock of God. In the Bible, God's people are many times called His sheep—*"We are His people and the sheep of His pasture"* (Psalm 100:3). The people of God collectively are called His flock.

> *Then he remembered the days of old, Moses and his people saying;*
>
> *"Where is He who brought them up out of the sea, with the shepherd of His flock?*
>
> *Where is He who put His Holy Spirit within them,*
>
> *Who led them by the right hand of Moses...?" (Isaiah 63:11, 12)*

Through Moses God led, guided, and provided for His flock as they came out of Egypt and made their way to the Promised Land. But it was not just the needs of the flock as a whole that the shepherd had to meet. There were individual and personal needs and disputes to be settled. The people came to Moses to seek guidance.

Jethro rightly discerned that the task needed more manpower. Taking his father-in-law's advice, Moses taught the moral and legal statutes that were to be Israel's standard, and he appointed under-shepherds—*"able men, such as fear God, men of truth, hating covetousness"*—to be *"rulers of thousands, rulers of hundreds, rulers of fifties, and rulers of tens"* (Exodus 18:21). They would deal with the lesser matters. The people of God no longer had to wait for a long time to receive counsel or justice; help was close at hand. Thus the principle of delegation and of sharing the load was set into the life of the people of God.

In the Church, the Body of Christ, shepherds, and under-shepherds are set in place, ministries recognized and developed, all working together to bring the Church to maturity as we come closer to our destiny—possession of the Land of Promise.

Jesus is the Chief Shepherd. He is the Good Shepherd who laid down His life for the sheep. Jesus said that His sheep know His voice. God's people have the Spirit who bears witness when truth is being spoken. More than ever, we need to be listening for the voice of the Shepherd.

Chapter 8. The Code in the Mount Sinai Experience—Fire from Heaven

Having redeemed and cleansed His people, the Lord of the Church equipped it to fulfill the Great Commission. Before Jesus ascended to Heaven, He commissioned the disciples to be His witnesses to the ends of the Earth and to make disciples of all the nations. He told them not to begin until they were *"endued with power from on high"* (Luke 24:49). The Holy Spirit, the "Promise of the Father," fell on the Feast of Pentecost, the anniversary of the giving of the Law at Mount Sinai.

Passover and Pentecost are two separate Feasts, fifty days apart. Passover brings us out of "Egypt" and Pentecost equips us for the work ahead. Jesus Himself is our pattern. Though born of the Spirit and sinless, He had to be endued with power by the Spirit before He began His ministry. All Christians have the Holy Spirit. When we trust in Christ as Saviour and Lord, we are born of the Spirit; but there is a special endowment of power given for ministry. We need a personal Pentecost to be as effective as we can be for the sake of the Kingdom. .

In the third month after the escape from Egypt, Israel came to the Wilderness of Sinai. The Pillar of Cloud settled on the mountain, and the people camped before it. Moses went up to God. All in all,

Moses was to ascend the mount eight times, speaking with God and delivering His messages to the people and, most importantly, receiving the Law and the design of the Tabernacle.

On this occasion, God announced His intention to make Israel a people above all people, His own special treasure. If they would agree to the Covenant which God would place before them, they would be a kingdom of priests, a holy nation. The people agreed, saying, *"All that the LORD has spoken we will do"* (Exodus 19:8), and sanctified themselves in preparation.

On the third day, there was fire and smoke on the mountain. It trembled as in an earthquake and there was the long loud blast of a trumpet—manifestations similar to those which occurred on the Day of Pentecost centuries later, when the Holy Spirit descended upon the hundred and twenty gathered in an upper room in Jerusalem.

Why did God wait until *"the Day of Pentecost had fully come"* (Acts 2:1), to pour out His Spirit on His Church? It was in fulfillment of the pattern that God Himself had set in Israel. Remember the principle of the Code: God's purposes are demonstrated in Israel, fulfilled in Christ, and manifested through the Church—first the Natural, then the Spiritual. At Mount Sinai, God equipped His people to do what He had called them to do. If they were to be a kingdom of priests and a holy nation, they would need His Law and the Tabernacle, where God could dwell in the midst of His people. On the Day of Pentecost as the infant Church assembled in that upper room, God inaugurated the Living Temple and wrote His Law on their hearts, as He declared through the Prophet Jeremiah: *"But this is the covenant that I will make with the house of Israel after those days, says the LORD: I will put My law in their minds, and write it on their hearts; and I will be their God and they shall be My people"* (Jeremiah 31:33).

The law that God writes in the hearts of His people is the law of love; *"...the love of God has been poured out in our hearts by the Holy Spirit who was given to us"* (Romans 5:5). Love for God and for our neighbor is the fulfillment of the law.

With the descent of the Spirit, the power of God came upon His people. The early Church went out and continued Jesus' work of destroying the works of the Devil. The Gospel was preached with power; healings, miracles, and deliverance from demons were frequent. The Church grew and expanded. The task of making disciples of all nations had begun. The experience at Mount Sinai was an indispensable part of God's preparation of His people Israel to fulfill their mission just as the experience of Pentecost continues to be for the Church.

The Law was given three times at Mount Sinai: once orally, spoken directly to the people from out of the fire and smoke on the mountain; then twice on tablets of stone, written by God Himself. Why twice?

Moses sojourned on the Mount with God for forty days and nights, during which time He was given the Law engraved on tablets of stone and also the design of the Tabernacle. The people tired of waiting for him and urged Aaron to make a golden calf to be their god. Though they had taken an oath of allegiance to serve the Lord, in such a short time they fell into idolatry.

Moses cast down the tablets of stone and broke them just as Israel had broken God's Law. The shattered pieces of the tablets symbolized man's inability to keep the Law of God. As a result three thousand people lost their lives as God executed judgment. By contrast, when the Spirit came on the Day of Pentecost, three thousand were baptized and added to the infant Church *"...for the letter* [of the Law] *kills, but the Spirit gives life"* (2 Corinthians 3:6).

Moses interceded for the people for forty days and nights and was again called up the Mount where he received a second set of tablets on which God wrote the Ten Commandments. This second set was placed in the Ark of the Covenant where they were kept. The Ark, with its Mercy Seat where God met with Man, is a type of the Lord Jesus. He kept the Law of God perfectly. The tablets of stone remained in the Ark, perfectly kept and perfectly safe.

The Law which was *"holy and just and good"* (Romans 7:12) could only condemn because Man could not keep it; but God's Son kept the Law and His righteousness is imputed to those who trust in Him. Along with the Law which brought death, God gave the Tabernacle which was a means of grace and forgiveness.

The Tabernacle—The Meeting Place of God and Man

The Tabernacle, with its wealth of imagery or representation of spiritual truths, needs a book to itself to even begin to do it justice. However, we cannot pass by without making some mention of it here. When Moses came down from the Mount with the first set of tablets, he also brought with him the plans of the Tabernacle. The Law alone could only bring death, because Man could not keep it, but the Tabernacle and its attendant sacrifices brought God's mercy and forgiveness and restored communion.

God told Moses to tell the people to bring offerings of precious stones, gold, silver, bronze, acacia wood, fine linen, and other materials, instructing, *"And let them make Me a sanctuary, that I may dwell among them"* (Exodus 25:8).

God had begun the process of restoring man's state as an entity made in the image of God and indwelt by God Himself. This was always God's plan for us. When God created Man, He breathed into him the breath of life, that is, He imparted into Man His own Spirit, and Man was joined to God—a living temple of the Spirit of God. When sin entered the human race, the Spirit of God departed and spiritual death came upon Man and death and decay upon all Creation.

Here at Mount Sinai, the separation was still there, but there was now a place where God could dwell in the midst of His people. The Tabernacle was to house the Ark of the Covenant, made of acacia wood overlaid with gold, with a lid of pure gold at each end of which was a golden cherub. This lid was called the Mercy Seat. God said to Moses:

"And there I will meet with you, and I will speak with you from above the mercy seat, from between the two cherubim which are on the ark of the Testimony, of all things which I will give you in commandment to the children of Israel." (Exodus 25:22)

Moses, as the Mediator of the Covenant, communed with God face to face, and Aaron as the High Priest could go before the Lord on the Day of Atonement. Under the Old Covenant this was as close as God and Man could be. God dwelt in the midst of His people with the tents of the Israelites camped around and He led them with the Pillar of Cloud and Fire; but to go into the Presence in the Holy of Holies meant death.

Then Jesus came! He was the Living Tabernacle of God. *"And the Word became flesh and dwelt* [literally 'tabernacled'] *among us and we beheld His glory, the glory as of the only begotten of the Father, full of grace and truth"* (John 1:14).

God came to be with us in a tent of human flesh. He was *Emmanuel*, meaning "God with us." Jesus came to live as Man was intended to be: human but holy, indwelt by God and in perfect communion with Him.

All of the furniture of the Tabernacle were representations of some aspect of the ministry of the One who was to come, but the Ark was the highest representation of Christ. It contained the unbroken Tablets of the Law, a golden pot of manna [the eternal Word of God], and Aaron's rod that budded [Resurrection Life in God's chosen High Priest].

The Ark resided in the innermost part of the Tabernacle behind a heavy veil. Over it hovered the *Shekinah*. From the outside there was nothing remarkable about the building itself. Only the Presence of God over it marked it as special. The curtains of the Outer Court were of pure white linen and the roof of the Tabernacle was made of grey badger skins. It was only as one entered that the beauty was revealed. There was a progression of light, from natural light in the Outer Court, to the light from the golden Lampstand in the Holy Place, and on into where the *Shekinah*—the Glory of God, was manifested in the Holy of Holies. There was also a progression of richness in the materials used in the furniture and curtains, from bronze and wood, to silver and gold, and the solid gold of the Lampstand and the Mercy Seat.

Like the Tabernacle, at first appearance, there was nothing very remarkable about Jesus. *"He has no form or comeliness; And when we see Him, There is no beauty that we should desire Him"* (Isaiah 53:2). To some He is just an ordinary man; to some a prophet or great teacher perhaps. It is only as we come to know Him and progress in that knowledge that His beauty is revealed. Paul, at a loss for adequate words, could say only *"Thanks be to God for His indescribable gift!"* (2 Corinthians 9:15).

I have read, though I have not been able to verify, that the entrances to the three compartments of the Tabernacle were literally called the Way, the Truth, and the Life and this certainly describes the experience of the three compartments of the Tabernacle. The Outer Court, lit by natural light, contained the bronze Altar of Sacrifice representing the Cross [the only Way to God], and also the Brazen Laver [the cleansing Word of God].

The Priestly Garment [the Holy Spirit] opens to us the Holy Place housing the golden Lampstand, Altar of Incense and Table of Showbread. This is a whole new dimension in God. Lit by the steady glow of the Lampstand it is for us the place of Truth, where the Holy Spirit brings a deepening communion with God and a growing revelation of His divine intents and purposes.

There is a deeper place with God yet to be entered into: that is the Holy of Holies beyond the Veil. Though the Veil was rent when Jesus died and legally there is nothing between us and God; when there is not a full revelation of the Cross, the Veil remains over our conscience. When that Veil is removed, the Life of the Resurrected Christ will flow freely through His people, bringing a healing stream to the people of the world.

The Tabernacle spells out the same pattern as shown in the Journey to the Promised Land. It too, in its three compartments, represents the truths of the Feasts of Passover, Pentecost and Tabernacles, but in a different form. The Journey is the Kingly walk where we learn to live out our identities as sons of the Living God, having authority over the enemy, and enforcing the victory of the King. The Tabernacle is the Priestly walk where we learn the fellowship of His sufferings and the power of His Resurrection. It is the Servant anointing to minister to lost humanity. We will reconsider the significance of the Veil further on.

The sacrifice of Jesus, our Passover Lamb, brought a cleansing whereby we could be declared holy and fit places for God to dwell. On the Day of Pentecost, fifty days after the Resurrection, God came to live IN His people. The Church is now the Body of Christ and the Temple of the Living God. The glories of the Tabernacle are such that we could linger for a long time, but in order to keep the continuity of the Journey, we must continue.

One year after leaving Egypt, the Tabernacle was raised up and the Glory of God filled it. Israel camped at the foot of Mount Sinai for about another year, the Tabernacle in the midst of the camp and the tribes camped around it in a prescribed and orderly manner, each tribe with its own standard. While they are thus camped, we will digress for a while to consider something of the history of the Church.

Israel at that point and the Church at this point in time have not fulfilled their God-given Commission though we have both reached the holy Mount and are traversing the wilderness beyond. We are a Royal Priesthood and a holy Nation with a destiny to fulfill. Ahead lies the Promised Land. Israel eventually did conquer the Land. Are we ready to conquer?

Chapter 9. The Code and the Restoration of the Church

The early Church, born on the day of Pentecost and nurtured by the Apostles, was a vital Church, bold in mission, moving in the power of the Holy Spirit. It was an evangelizing force which *"turned the world upside down"* (Acts 17:6).

Surviving persecution and the early inroads of heresy, the Church eventually became acceptable when the Emperor Constantine embraced Christianity in 312 AD. Many who had never had a true conversion joined the Church, swelling the numbers but reducing its spirituality, and though there have always been those who have lived close to God, the Church at large succumbed to apathy and error and became increasingly institutional and ritualistic. During the "Dark Ages," the light of the Gospel was almost obscured. The Scriptures were lost to the common people; heathen practices and immorality were tolerated.

In the Book of Samuel is a story which exemplifies the state of the Church during this time. The Ark of the Covenant—over which the *Shekinah*, or Glory of God, was manifested and which belonged in the Holy of Holies in the Tabernacle—was captured by the Philistines. On hearing the news, Eli the High Priest died. His daughter-in-law at that time was delivered of a son. She called him *Ichabod*, meaning "the

Glory has departed." Though there was always a remnant of faithful people, the Church of the Dark Ages was an Ichabod institution. There is a story of a saint who was being shown over the Vatican. Pointing to the rich treasures which the Church possessed, the Pope said, "No longer can we say 'Silver and gold have I none.' "No, sire," said the saint, "Neither can we say, 'Rise up and walk.'"

The Church, like the first generation of Israel from Egypt, failed to fulfill its destiny. Unbelief and rebellion doomed the People of God to wilderness wanderings. But God hadn't finished with Israel, and today the Church is still His instrument of restoration to the Earth. A generation arose in Israel that completed the Journey. Led by Joshua, they conquered the enemy and eventually Israel established the kingdom with the Son of David on the throne. Even now in the Church, God is raising up a "Joshua" generation that will overcome the enemy, complete the Great Commission, and prepare the way for Jesus, the Greater Son of David, to return and rule.

> *God is raising up a Joshua generation...*

When God began restoring the Church, He first raised up men like Huss and Tyndale to make His Word available to the people. The Spirit and the Word began to bring to light again truths that had been lost for centuries.

The first truth restored in the 1500s, mainly through Martin Luther, was Justification by faith—faith in Jesus the Lamb of God who takes away the sin of the world. In the Wesleyan revival in the 1700s the truth of Justification by faith was re-emphasized and the truth of Sanctification was restored. In the 1900s, in the Pentecostal and Charismatic Renewals, God restored the truth of the Empowering of the Holy Spirit.

For centuries God has guided the Church on its journey toward its destiny. He brought us out of "Egypt" [the kingdom of darkness] by the shed blood of the Passover Lamb [Jesus)] We were slaves of

"Pharaoh" [Satan] but have been brought out from under his authority, sanctified, declared holy, and set apart to God. At Pentecost He equipped the Church to fulfill its Commission and He will bring us into the Land a conquering army. What has been demonstrated in Israel will be manifested in the Church through the power of the Cross of Christ.

It is clear that in bringing the Church to the fulfillment of its earthly mission, God is restoring it according to the pattern in the types. We have had our Passovers and our Pentecosts. Ahead is the Feast of Tabernacles, the feast of fullness or completion, which has never been fulfilled in the Church. Though instructions for this Feast were given in the wilderness, the first time it is recorded as being celebrated was at the dedication of the Temple when Israel had completed their mission.

The Pattern Repeated in the Life of Jesus

According to our code, God's purposes are first of all demonstrated in Israel. Into that nation's history He established a pattern, or drafted a map, which revealed the principles whereby He, through His people, would bring Restoration to the Earth. That pattern, or map, remained as the blueprint for Operation Restore. It is, as we said, a physical map of a spiritual journey.

God called the nation of Israel His "Son." This Son, as we have seen, had a commission to fulfill. When Jesus, the only begotten Son of God, came into the world, He also came with a mission: *"For this purpose the Son of God was manifested, that He might destroy the works of the devil"* (1 John 3:8).

It was the works of the devil that spoiled this planet. Things were about to change.

Jesus came to take back the authority which the devil had usurped from Adam. In the preparation for His ministry, Jesus' life followed the pattern which God had laid down in the life of the nation:

Brought out of Egypt in infancy

"When Israel was a child I loved him, and out of Egypt I called my son" (Hosea 11:1);

Matthew, in recording Joseph and Mary's flight into Egypt with the infant Jesus, applies this Scripture to Jesus (Matthew 2:14, 15).

> *When he arose, he took the young Child and His mother by night and departed for Egypt, And was there until the death of Herod, that it might be fulfilled which was spoken by the Lord through the prophet, saying "Out of Egypt I called My Son."*

<u>Set apart to God</u>

The nation sanctified then baptized in the Red Sea;
Jesus consecrated by baptism in the River Jordan.

<u>Equipped for mission</u>

The Nation equipped with the Law and the Tabernacle at Mount Sinai;
Jesus equipped with the Holy Spirit.

<u>Tested in the Wilderness</u>

The nation had forty years of wilderness wanderings;
Jesus in the wilderness forty days.

<u>Fulfilling the Commission</u>

The nation came out of the wilderness and began to defeat the enemy and possess the Land;
Jesus came out of the wilderness *"in the power of the Spirit"* (Luke 4:14) and began to destroy the works of the devil and demonstrate the Kingdom.

This is the pattern which God has set in the Scriptures for the Church to follow. The Body of Christ, with Jesus as the Head, is the corporate Son of God—*"...as He is, so are we in this world"* (1 John 4:17).

Whatever Jesus is so are we in this world. We travel the same journey as Jesus and the Nation of Israel. It is the journey of the Sons of God as they walk into their divinely ordained destiny.

Summary of the Sons of God in Restoration
(See Illustration)

The Corporate Son—the Nation of Israel

Father Abraham gave his son to God on Mount Moriah. God told him, *"in Isaac your seed shall be called"* (Genesis 21:12). The people who sprang from Isaac God called His "Son." Through this Son God would demonstrate, in the natural realm, what He would do in the spiritual realm in restoring the Earth. Their mission was to possess the land of Canaan and establish the Kingdom.

The Only-Begotten Son, Jesus

Because Abraham did not withhold his son from God, God blessed the Earth by giving us His Son. Jesus is the One who makes it all possible. His mission was to destroy the works of the Devil. Through His one offering for all people for all time, He satisfied the legal demands of the Law and silenced the Accuser. His redeemed people are born of the Spirit, and are joint heirs with Him. Jesus' preparation for ministry followed the pattern of the Journey to the Promised Land. Then He went to the Cross to make a way for us to take the spiritual journey which leads to the establishment of the Kingdom of God on Earth as it is in Heaven.

The Corporate Spiritual Son, the Church

Jesus is the Head of this corporate Son as Isaac was the head of Israel. Our mission is to make disciples of all the nations, i.e., to possess the Earth and establish the Kingdom. Jesus will then return to reign.

In the journey of the Church we have yet to come out of the wilderness and conquer the Land. How we do that is revealed in the code.

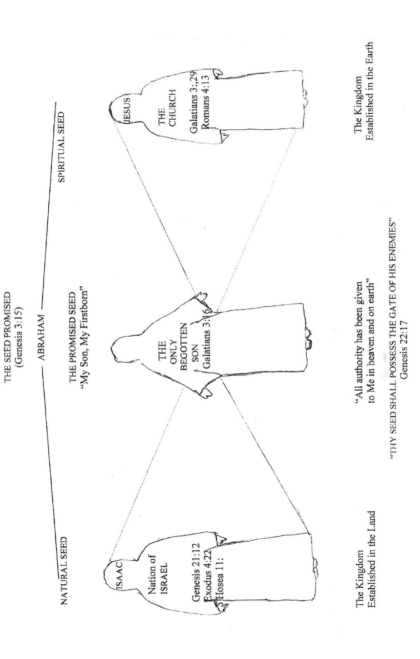

THE SEED PROMISED
(Genesis 3:15)

ABRAHAM

NATURAL SEED

SPIRITUAL SEED

THE PROMISED SEED
"My Son, My Firstborn"

JESUS

THE
CHURCH

Galatians 3:29
Romans 4:13

THE
ONLY
BEGOTTEN
SON
Galatians 3:16

ISAAC

Nation of
ISRAEL

Genesis 21:12
Exodus 4:22
Hosea 11:

The Kingdom
Established in the Earth

"All authority has been given
to Me in heaven and on earth"

"THY SEED SHALL POSSESS THE GATE OF HIS ENEMIES"
Genesis 22:17

The Kingdom
Established in the Land

77

Chapter 10. Truths That Triumph Over the Wilderness

Negotiating the wilderness was a necessary part of the training of the People of God. The wilderness weans us from the ways of Egypt and teaches us total dependence on God. Remember the purpose of the wilderness as stated in Deuteronomy 8:2, 3:

> *"And you shall remember that the Lord your God led you all the way these forty years in the wilderness, to humble you and test you, to know what was in your heart, whether you would keep His commandments or not.*
>
> *So He humbled you, allowed you to hunger, and fed you with manna which you did not know nor did your fathers know, that He might make you know that man shall not live by bread alone; but man lives by every word that proceeds from the mouth of the LORD."*

In other words: Are we going to believe God or not? Are we going to act out of the Word of God or out of what we see and feel and what the world, the flesh, and the devil are saying? It is the same test that Eve faced in the Garden. We lost Eden through unbelief; restoration comes through faith. Eden was without doubt a physical place, but it was first and foremost a spiritual state where Man lived in full communion with God. In Christ the spiritual state of Eden is restored. When we realize that and learn to rest in Him, then we are ready to possess the Land and the beauty of Eden will be restored to the Earth. When God created the world, He began with the Heavens and the Earth and finished with the Creation of Man. In restoring the Earth, He begins with the New Man and ends with the renewed Heavens and Earth.

The Garden of Grace and the Wilderness of Works

Eden was the Garden of Grace. Man lived in unbroken communion with God and everything was supplied by Him. Man opened his eyes on a finished Creation. He was to tend and keep and have dominion over the works of God's hands. When Man decided to go his own way, he was banished from Eden and entered the Wilderness of Works. Works is about who you are and what you can do apart from God.

It is the realm where the relentless Accuser accuses us day and night because we can never measure up. In the wilderness we wrestle for survival by the sweat of our brow.

While Christians know that we are saved by grace through faith, too often our understanding is a mixture of grace and works. It is like riding a lift halfway up a skyscraper, then getting out to labor up the stairs for the rest of the way because "Praise God! Jesus has saved me and forgiven me but now it is all up to me." The good news is that the lift goes all the way up. The lift is called "Life in Christ Jesus" (Romans 8:2) and it's powered by grace. It represents the redemptive work of Christ. You can rest in it, sit in it, lie down in it, and even sleep in it. The lift will take you all the way to the finish. Paul writes to the Galatians who got caught in the "works" trap: *"Are you so foolish? Having begun in the Spirit, are you now being made perfect by the flesh?"* (Galatians 3:3).

God's grace is pre-venient, i.e., it goes before us. Our salvation begins by grace through faith and it is grace through faith all the way. This is what the Sabbath rest is all about. It is not a rest of inactivity. Ephesians 2:9 tells us that God has prepared good works for us to do. It is the heart- rest of faith, knowing and operating out of, our position in Christ.

The writer to the Hebrews in writing about Israel's failure to enter the Land through unbelief says:

There remains therefore a rest for the people of God.

For he who has entered His rest has himself also ceased from his works as God did from His. Let us therefore be diligent to enter that rest, lest anyone fall after the same example of disobedience." (Hebrews 4:9–11)

We are not ready to enter the Land until we have learned to rest in grace. Only on the basis of Christ's finished work can we hope to conquer the enemy.

The Brazen Serpent

As the people journeyed from Mount Hor, there was an incident which again depicts the principle of grace. Here we see clearly how a physical happening in the Old Testament portrays a spiritual reality in the New Testament.

The people became dispirited and resorted to grumbling and complaining. God sent fiery serpents among them and many died. The people repented and confessed their sin and asked Moses to pray for them. God told Moses to make a bronze serpent and put it on a pole. Those who looked at it were healed. All they had to do was to look at the brazen serpent—the representation of that from which they were dying.

Jesus referred to this incident when Nicodemus came to enquire of Him. He said, *"And as Moses lifted up the serpent in the wilderness, even so must the Son of Man be lifted up, that whoever believes in Him should not perish but have eternal life"* (John 3:14, 15).

The serpent in Scripture is a symbol of sin. Jesus became sin for us: *"For He made Him who knew no sin to be sin for us, that we might become the righteousness of God in Him"* (2 Corinthians 5:21).

We, too, are dying from the bite of the serpent. Just by looking in faith to Jesus lifted up on the Cross bearing our sins, we are delivered from death and declared to be the righteousness of God in Christ.

An evangelist gave a graphic illustration of this. He told of an artist who painted the scene from the incident recorded in Numbers 21. In the centre of the picture was the bronze serpent on a pole; above and beyond it was Jesus on the Cross. On the ground were fiery serpents among the people. To one side were two men. One of the men was trying to get his dying friend to look at the serpent on the pole, but the doomed man's face was livid with rage, his arms flailing as he stubbornly refused to look. He died, arguing.

Another man was kneeling in prayer. This surely is a very good thing to do, but his back was turned to the pole. He died, being religious.

There was another man engaged in a valiant struggle with the serpents. He had one by the throat and looked as though he had the better of it, but while he was wrestling that one, another serpent came from behind and bit him on the ankle. He died, doing his best.

In the foreground was a mother holding a little girl who had been bitten. The mother had turned the child to face the brazen serpent on the pole and was pointing the child to it. She lived, believing.

> *...unless you are converted and become as little children, you will by no means enter the kingdom of heaven. (Matthew 18:3)*

> *...the message of the Cross is [still] foolishness to those who are perishing. (1 Corinthians 1:18)* {

In our human pride we like to think that our efforts—our intelligence, our piousness, our anything else that gives us credit— is indispensable. So we die in the Wilderness of Works because possession of the Land is on the merit of Christ's work alone, not ours. It is <u>always</u> by grace through faith.

Our code supplies us with another graphic illustration of grace through faith in the incident at Kadesh. Again, as at Horeb, there was no water and the people thirsted. As before, God would provide water from a rock. This time, however, instead of smiting the rock, Moses was told to just speak to the rock.

Remember that, in type, the Rock was Christ, as in 1 Corinthians 10:4: *"For they drank of that spiritual Rock that followed them, and that Rock was Christ."* Moses, angry at the murmuring of the people, struck the Rock twice and said, *"Hear now, you rebels! Must we bring water for you out of this rock?"* (Numbers 20:10; emphasis added).

Psalm 106:33 says that he spoke rashly with his lips. Moses was boasting of his own ability to produce the water. Redemption is never of man's works, *"lest anyone should boast"* (Ephesians 2:9). The rock yielded water, but Moses disqualified himself from entering the Land.

It is commonly taught that it was disobedience that kept him out, but primarily it was unbelief. God said: *"Because you did not believe Me, to hallow Me in the eyes of the children of Israel, therefore you shall not bring this congregation into the land which I have given them"* (Numbers 20:12; emphasis added). Moses' action did not honour God or give Him the glory. Instead he claimed credit for himself.

Disobedience follows unbelief. If we believe then we obey. Moses, the Mediator of the Law and typical of the Law, couldn't believe that a bit of human effort wasn't necessary. It was all up to him. He had to bring water out of the rock. The Law was about what we can do. Grace is about what God has done for us through Christ.

Probably we have all thought that Moses' punishment was a bit harsh, after all the years of faithful commitment, but remember that God was laying down a principle here. He was leaving a vital clue for us "on whom the ends of the ages have come."

That Rock was Christ. One smiting of the Rock was sufficient. It was all that was necessary to give access to all the provision of God. We need only to speak to the Rock. What is speaking to the Rock? It is prayer, praise and our faith confession of the Word. It's not our works which make the fountain flow; it's faith in His finished work. By prayer and our faith confession we appropriate what has already been done for us at the Cross. Praise and thanksgiving affirm our faith in Him.

Moses was indeed a great man of God. He came a long way by faith but couldn't enter into the Land because he lapsed into trusting in his own works. Did he make it into Heaven? Certainly! In Matthew 17 we see him on the Mount of Transfiguration with Elijah, talking to Jesus. As we have stated, entering the Land isn't about going to Heaven. It's about fulfilling the mission of the Church here on Earth.

Moses learned his lesson. At the border of the Promised Land he warned Israel not to think that they would possess the Land because of *their* righteousness, but because of the wickedness of the inhabitants and because of God's promise to Abraham Isaac and Jacob. *"Therefore understand that the LORD your God is not giving you this good land to possess because of your righteousness, for you are a stiff-necked people"* (Deuteronomy 9:6).

To conquer the Land we need to see that one smiting of the Rock is enough, i.e., the Cross is all-sufficient. In many and subtle ways we keep smiting the Rock. When we say that Jesus has yet more to do before the Kingdom is established, we are smiting the Rock. We are saying that the Cross wasn't enough. The Scriptures say that Jesus is now seated at the Father's right hand, waiting for His enemies to be made His footstool. Jesus will come again when we have completed our assignment to make disciples of all the nations, and by grace through faith, we have put His enemies under His feet.

When we say that we have to "die to self" then we are smiting the Rock. It sounds very pious and commendable, but plainly it is works. Jesus has already done the job:

I have been crucified with Christ. (Galatians 2:20; emphasis added)

For you died, and your life is hidden with Christ in God. (Colossians 3:3; emphasis added)

If One died for all, then all died. (2 Corinthians 5:14; emphasis added)

...knowing this, that our old man was crucified with Him that the body of sin might be done away with. (Romans 6:6; emphasis added)

And those who are Christ's have crucified the flesh with its passions and desires. (Galatians 5:24; emphasis added)

> **We do not need to wrestle with flesh and blood, including our own; that battle has been won.**

We need to stop smiting the Rock and learn to rest in His completed work on our behalf. As Paul says in Romans 6:11, "Consider it done." By ONE offering He has perfected us forever (Hebrews 10:14). But doesn't Paul say, "I die daily" (1 Corinthians 15:31)? In the context he is talking about the perils he faces daily for the sake of the Gospel. The Accuser will keep us busy wrestling the flesh, smiting the Rock. It's a red herring, a delaying tactic, to keep us from doing what we're supposed to be doing—wrestling against powers and principalities and spiritual wickedness in the heavenlies and liberating the Earth from Satan's grip. We do not need to wrestle with flesh and blood, including our own; that battle has been won. The new dynamic of the Spirit is at work in our lives and we can choose to stand in our position in Christ

The battle against the enemy will be won only on the basis of what Jesus has done, not on the basis of what we can do. We do, however, need to consecrate ourselves and be totally available to God. That shouldn't be difficult when we see what's at stake and the glorious victory ahead.

How then are we changed into Christ's image if not by battling the flesh? 2 Corinthians 3:18 gives the answer: *"But we all, with unveiled face, beholding, as in a mirror the glory of the Lord, are being transformed into the same image from glory to glory, just as by the Spirit of the Lord."*

We are changed through revelation. Every time the Spirit shows us more of Him a change is effected in us because it is a spiritual principle that no man can see God and live (Exodus 33:20). At each glimpse of His glory, something of the old nature in us dies as the hush of holiness settles in our soul and silences Self. Jacob saw God face to face at Peniel and thereafter he walked with a limp. No longer did he have confidence in himself, only in God. As Paul was to say centuries later, *"Our sufficiency is from God"* (2 Corinthians 3:5).

You can tell when people have seen God; it shows. Moses saw God and his face shone with glory. Isaiah saw God in the temple and was thereafter totally committed to Him. Head knowledge can make us proud, even just head knowledge of the Bible: *"Knowledge puffs up"* (1 Corinthians 8:1). But a revelation of God humbles us. When we see God's glory with the eyes of our heart, the flesh is dumb—there's nothing to say. Job saw God and didn't need answers anymore. Seeing God was enough. He said:

I have heard of You by the hearing of the ear,

But now my eye sees You.

Therefore I abhor myself,

And repent in dust and ashes. (Job 42:5, 6)

It is seeing the goodness of God that leads us to repentance (Romans 2:4). When Moses asked to see God, He said, *"I will make all My goodness pass before you, and I will proclaim the name of the LORD before you"* (Exodus 33:19). Moses received a revelation of a merciful, gracious, longsuffering God abounding in goodness and truth, and his face reflected His glory. Supremely, God is revealed in His Son Jesus: *"...God...has shone in our hearts to give the light of the knowledge of the glory of God in the face of Jesus Christ"* (2 Corinthians 4:6).

It is a humbling, purifying experience to see God. If we want to be like Jesus all we need to do is to seek His face, and we will be changed from glory to glory. Legally, our old nature died at the Cross; it was crucified with Christ. Experientially, day by day, we are changed by revelation. We are responsible, of course, to walk in the light of what we have seen.

"...For everyone to whom much is given, from him much will be required...". (Luke 12:48)

The Mystery of the Veil

The *Shekinah*—the Glory of God—in the Holy of Holies in the Tabernacle, and later in the Temple, was hidden behind a heavy veil woven with cherubim, reminiscent of the cherubim which guarded the entrance to Eden and the Tree of Life. To enter meant death. Hebrews tells us that the veil was His (Christ's) flesh; and 1 Peter 2:24 says that Jesus *"Himself bore our sins, in His own body on the tree."* It was our sins which separated us from God and those sins were placed on His body—the *"veil, that is, His flesh"* (Hebrews 10:20).

At the moment of Christ's death the Veil was torn from top to bottom, showing that all that separated us from God has been done away with forever.

Most Christians know that the veil was taken away and that we can now come boldly to the throne of Grace. However for many of God's people sin-consciousness remains because they don't have a revelation of the completeness and permanence of the removal of sin; therefore for them a Veil remains. The Accuser constantly directs our attention to our imperfections. As long as our eyes are on them, he has power over us. When we see that every one of our sins, past present and future are woven into that Veil and the Veil has been torn apart as Christ's body was broken for us, then we see beyond the Veil to the *Shekinah*—the glory of God. The guardian cherubim sheathe their flaming swords and Eden opens to us. No more hiding behind bushes as the guilty Adam did. The Accuser's voice is silenced. Jesus said that the pure in heart will see God (Matthew 5:8). The pure in heart are those who know without doubt that their sins have been removed and they are in full communion with God.

The Restoring Army that God is raising will be a people who have seen God. They have Eden in their hearts and their burning desire is to see its blessedness extended to the whole Earth. They have seen that the battle against flesh and blood has been won, and they are ready to do battle against the powers, and principalities and spiritual wickedness in the heavenlies.

Jesus is often referred to as "the second Adam," to teach that Christ is the new Head of the human race. All who are redeemed are in Him and are part of the New Creation. That much is gloriously true. However it tells only half the story. The Bible nowhere refers to Jesus as the second Adam but "the last Adam" and "the second Man" (1 Corinthians 15:45–47). As the last Adam, He gathered into Himself all the ruin of Adam's race.

The trial of Jesus was much more than an earthly trial. The Courts of Heaven were in session. Jesus stood silently in the dock, offering no defense because He was bearing the sins of all humanity, past, present, and future. The condemnation of every age was resting on Him. "Adam" was judged, found to be guilty, executed, and buried. That was the last of Adam with all of his sin and imperfections. The price has been fully paid. As far as God is concerned Adam is no more. That is the significance of "the last Adam."

Jesus rose as "the second Man," the Lord from Heaven, Head of the new breed of Man. This new breed of Man is born from above, free from all condemnation, bearing the image of the heavenly Man, heirs of God and joint-heirs with Christ, perfected forever in the sight of God.

The sacrifice of Jesus has brought us from the lowest to the highest; from bondage to sin, death, and condemnation into being heirs of God with throne rights and having Kingdom authority. Jesus stripped Satan of all his power over us and restored dominion to us. We have yet to enter into the full exercise of that dominion.

As we have seen, the first generation of Israel failed the wilderness test. God called Israel "My Son." He redeemed them, guided them, provided for them, equipped them, and dwelt in the midst of them. He called them to be a Kingdom of priests and a Holy Nation. He took them to the borders of the Promised Land and told them to go in and conquer. He promised to be with them and they would be victorious. Their faith confession was "We're just grasshoppers."

In the wilderness, the question of Son-ship has to be settled. Are we who God says we are and can we do what He says we can do? Are we grasshoppers, or are we Overcomers—slaves or Sons?

At the River Jordan as the Holy Spirit descended upon Jesus, the Father declared, *"You are My beloved Son; in You I am well pleased"* (Luke 3:12). The tempter challenged, *"IF you are the Son of God..."* (Luke 4:3; emphasis added), echoing the sneer in Eden: *"Did God really say...?"* Jesus knew who He was. He didn't have to prove it to anyone. He fought every temptation with the Word and came out of the wilderness in the power of the Spirit. He then began to demolish the strongholds of the enemy.

The second generation of Israel from Egypt stood poised to enter and possess the Land. God had said that the old generation must die before Israel could enter. We are ready to enter when we see that what the Bible calls our "old man" (Romans 6:6) is dead. He was condemned and crucified with Christ and we have a new identity, risen with Christ, having Kingdom authority. Out in the wilderness, day by day, Israel saw the old men die. Moses their leader was also dead, and it was no coincidence that the new leader was called *Joshua*—this is the Old Testament name for Jesus. He was to accomplish what Moses could not.

For what the law could not do in that it was weak through the flesh, God did by sending His own Son... (Romans 8:3)

But...Joshua...he shall go over before this people, and he shall cause them to inherit the land which you will see. (Deuteronomy 3:28)

Jesus, our Joshua, has gone over before us and, by the power of His resurrection life in us, He will cause us to inherit the Land.

The old nature, like the old generation of Israel, is dogged by doubt and disobedience. It clings to the slave mentality of "Egypt" and cannot overcome. It is governed by what it sees and experiences in the material world *"by bread alone."* The good news is that the old Man is dead, and the new Man in Christ is an Overcomer. I've heard it said that when Watchman Nee came into that revelation, he ran down the street shouting "I'm dead, I'm dead, Praise God I'm dead."

The new generation of Israel that emerged from the wilderness had seen the old men die and all that was of Egypt was left behind. They had learned to live by faith—by believing that what God said was true. They were ready to overcome all obstacles by the power of the Word, *"...by every word that proceeds from the mouth of God"* (Deuteronomy 8:3).

Chapter 11. The Code Reveals New Territory Ahead

Jesus came out of the wilderness *"in the power of the Spirit"* and began to destroy the works of the devil. Israel came out of the wilderness fully prepared for the battle ahead and the hosts of Heaven joined them. The Church is about to come out of the wilderness in the power of the Spirit. How can we know that? Every truth which is encoded in the type of Israel's journey to the Promised Land, up to this point, has been restored to the Church. New truth will take us into new territory.

The Church, on its spiritual journey, has advanced by revelation of the Word. As Jesus promised, the Spirit, like the Cloud of Glory, has gone before us to lead and guide into all truth and show us things to come. All revelation has brought a deeper understanding of what was accomplished at the Cross. Not everyone could receive new revelation, but those who did moved on. New truth opens up new horizons—new possibilities in God, not just for ourselves, but for the whole Earth.

Listen as God instructs His people at the borders of the Promised Land:

When you see the ark of the covenant of the LORD your God, and the priests, the Levites, bearing it, then you shall set out from your place and go after it.

Yet there shall be a <u>space between you and it, about two thousand cubits</u> by measure. Do not come near it, that you may know the way by which you must go, <u>for you have not passed this way before.</u>

And Joshua said to the people, "<u>Sanctify yourselves,</u> for tomorrow the LORD will do wonders among you." (Joshua 3:3–5; emphasis added)

The Church is about to enter new territory. It will go beyond where it has ever been. It is a way we have never passed before. That's a big statement when we think of the early Church as it proclaimed the gospel with power and with signs following, so that they were known as *"These who have turned the world upside down"* (Acts 17:6).

> **The Church is about to enter new territory…. a way we have never passed before.**

At this exciting, vital stage of the Journey, let's check our instructions:

* <u>Watch the Ark</u> so that we will know which way to go.

The Ark of the Covenant was the highest type of Christ that was in the Tabernacle. It contained the unbroken tablets of the Law - total righteousness, Aaron's rod that budded – Resurrection Life and The Golden Pot of Manna – The Bread of Life [the Word of God]. Over it, the cloud of Glory rested. We are to keep our eyes on Jesus. He is the One Who reveals the way ahead. As we have seen, Jesus came out of the wilderness and began to demolish the enemy's strongholds.

The Ark was to precede the Army of Israel by about two thousand cubits. ABOUT TWO THOUSAND YEARS AFTER JESUS CAME OUT OF THE WILDERNESS IN THE POWER OF THE SPIRIT, THE CHURCH WILL FOLLOW. Glory to God! That's soon. Jesus was about thirty years old when He came out of the wilderness (Luke 3:23). This was the age when those designated for the priesthood began their ministry. Since some miscalculations occurred in setting up our present calendar, we don't know exactly which year that would have been; also, the Scripture says about two thousand cubits. It can't be long. Get ready! The Joshua generation is here!

* Sanctify yourselves.

Consecrate yourselves; be dedicated to the cause of Christ. A mighty battle lies ahead—the greatest battle of all time; so much depends on it and discipline is called for.

> *You therefore must endure hardship as a good soldier of Jesus Christ.*

> *No one engaged in warfare entangles himself with the affairs of this life that he may please him who enlisted him as a soldier. (2 Timothy 2:3, 4)*

When the army of Israel was intimidated by the Philistine champion Goliath, David took up the challenge. He said, *"Is there not a cause?"* (1 Samuel 17:29). Is there not a cause? The ravages of the usurper are increasing in the earth: distress of nations, lawlessness, blatant anti-God amorality, daily massacre of the unborn. Creation is travailing and groaning, waiting for the manifestation of the sons of God. Romans 8:19–22 tells us that Creation is waiting to be delivered from corruption into the glorious liberty of the children of God, and it's the children of God who will do it. Yes, there is a cause! It is the highest cause there is.

Much of the popular end-time teaching magnifies the success of the enemy but offers little solution except to look for an imminent Rapture.

The problems are immense and, humanly speaking, insurmountable, but the power of the Cross is greater. David faced the huge Philistine and said, *"You come to me with a sword, with a spear, and with a javelin. But I come to you in the name of the LORD of hosts, the God of the armies of Israel, whom you have defied"* (1 Samuel 17:45).

And the rest, as they say, is history. No matter how large the enemy looms or how terrifying his weapons, they are no match for the LORD of hosts.

No weapon formed against you shall prosper,

And every tongue which rises against you in judgment

You shall condemn.

This is the heritage of the servants of the LORD,

And their righteousness is from Me, says the LORD." (Isaiah 54:17)

Wedding or War?

Much of the Church, following the popular teaching of an imminent Rapture, is getting ready for a Wedding and there is a lot of talk about the Bride. The marriage supper of the Lamb is certainly on the agenda; but not yet. This is the day of warfare and the warrior. There is, as you would agree, a big difference in getting ready for a wedding and getting ready for a war, so it's important that we get our end-time understanding right. Do I believe in a Rapture? I certainly do because the Bible teaches it; but more on that later.

The Jordan Crossing

The Jordan crossing ended the wanderings in the wilderness, just as the Red Sea crossing ended the slavery in Egypt. It was time to leave the wilderness behind and move on. The River Jordan was in flood, but that would not deter the advancing army. Rather, God used the flooded River to again leave vital clues. These truths would reinforce the truth of the completeness of the deliverance of the people of God.

All through the wilderness doubt had lingered. Were they really who God said they were: His Son? Could they bring down the giants and their mighty strongholds? Finally, doubt died along with the old men and truth triumphed. It could be done! The new generation was to see again the finality of their bondage to Egypt, understand their status as God's Son and Executer of His will, and enter into the reality of the Land.

> *"And it shall come to pass, as soon as the soles of the feet of the priests who bear the ark of the LORD, the Lord of all the earth, shall rest in the waters of the Jordan, that the waters of the Jordan shall be cut off, the waters that come down from upstream, and they shall stand as a heap." (Joshua 3:13)*

As we have seen, a "rest" in Scripture means a finished work. *"Let us therefore be diligent to enter that rest..."* (Hebrews 4:11).

As the feet of the priests carrying the Ark touched the swollen waters of the Jordan, the waters were cut off and rolled back as far as a city called Adam. That was no coincidence! The effects of the Cross go right back to Adam; it covers all Mankind.

The Ark, on the shoulders of the priests, led the way then rested in the middle of the River until all Israel had crossed over. As the people filed past the Ark, Israel in type entered into His rest or finished work. Twelve stones, one for each tribe, were taken from that resting place to build a memorial on Canaan's side and twelve stones from the wilderness side were placed in the midst of the Jordan where the Ark had rested. At the resting place of the Ark, the old was buried, and the new emerged. The priests bore the Ark to Canaan's side, the waters flowed again, and the past with its doubt and disobedience and its attachment to Egypt was gone forever.

The Church crosses Jordan when we see that all the bondage of "Egypt" has been buried with Jesus and we learn to stand in, and operate out of, our identity in the risen Christ. From the tomb of Christ the New Creation emerged. The Jordan brings a deeper revelation of just what took place at the Cross, the magnitude of our salvation and the unequivocal Grace of God. In answer to the apostle's prayer, we understand the hope to which He has called us and how rich is His glorious inheritance, and how great is His power in us and for us and the dominion over the powers of darkness, which has been restored to us. We are ready for war!

The Jordan crossing took place on the tenth day of the first month, the day of the choosing of the Passover Lamb forty years before. This speaks further of the identification of God's people with Christ our Passover. On this day they entered into all that was theirs through the sacrifice of the Passover Lamb in Egypt. At this same place centuries later, Jesus was immersed in baptism in identification with those He came to save. During the consecration of a priest according to the tabernacle rituals, the candidate was washed in the Laver, anointed with oil, and clothed with the priestly garment. Here at the Jordan, Jesus presented Himself to John the Baptist as a candidate for our great High Priest, the One Who would carry the burden of the people.

At Gilgal, Israel renewed the rite of circumcision, the seal of the Abrahamic Covenant. God said, *"This day I have rolled away the reproach of Egypt from you"* (Joshua 5:9). Nothing of "Egypt" remained. The transformation from slaves into conquerors was complete. The first Passover in the Land was celebrated, the manna ceased, and Israel ate of the produce of the Land.

Chapter 12. The Code in Conquest

At the entrance to the Promised Land stood the formidable-looking city of Jericho with its towering walls. In order to possess the Promised Land, Jericho had to be taken. As we see the obstacles ahead of us, we encourage ourselves by remembering God's promises to Father Abraham. In Genesis 22:17 we read, *"Your descendants shall possess the gate of their enemies."* The KJV renders this in the singular: *"Thy seed shall possess the gate of his enemies."* As we have seen, the promised Seed is one but many (see Galatians 3:16 and 29).

God saw the nation as one, a corporate body which He called "My Son." This corporate Son, which is the nation, and His only-begotten Son, Jesus, prevailed over the enemy. They both came out of the wilderness in the power of the Spirit and exercised Kingdom authority. They both completed their mission in the Earth. Victory over the enemy has been demonstrated in Israel and fulfilled in Christ. Now it's time for that victory to be manifested through the Church—the spiritual Son, the corporate Body of Christ. Jesus said,

> *"...on this rock I will build My Church and the gates of Hades will not prevail against it. And I will give you the keys of the kingdom of heaven, and whatever you bind on earth will be bound in heaven, and whatever you loose on earth will be loosed in heaven." (Matthew 16:18, 19)*

In the past we have understood this to mean that Satan and his hordes can never overcome the Church. That certainly is true. The Church of Jesus Christ has stood and grown in the face of every attack by the enemy. However, in the light of the promise made to Abraham, this interpretation falls short of the real intent of Jesus' declaration. Abraham's Seed is to *"possess the gate of their enemies."* That puts us on the attack, not on the defensive. The Church of Jesus Christ is to destroy the gates of Hell.

The *"ruler of this world"* is the prince of darkness, and Hell has invaded the Earth. The Church is here to demolish Hell's grip on the Earth. We have been given authority to bind and loose on Earth that which Jesus has already bound and loosed in Heaven or in the realm of the Spirit. As we have seen in Chapter 1, the reconciliation of all things has already been accomplished in seed form at the Cross. There, all things contrary to the Kingdom were bound and all Creation was set free and reconciled to God (Colossians 1:19, 20). This has yet to be manifested.

> **The Church of Jesus Christ is to destroy the Gates of Hell**

Jesus came to destroy the works of the devil (1 John 3:8). He is the Head of the Church and the Head has to do with authority. Jesus as Man's representative regained the authority which Satan usurped, and He has delegated it to His Church. He said, *"All authority in Heaven and Earth has been given to Me in heaven and on earth. Go therefore and make disciples of all the nations"* (Matthew 28:18, 19).

In order to bring the nations in, we have to do battle with the enemy. We have to bind and loose those things which Jesus has already legally bound and loosed at the Cross. The battleground is prayer. Prayer brings down the walls. Many people may not be aware that it was prayer which brought down the Iron Curtain, the Berlin wall, and the walls of apartheid in Africa. As God's people faithfully prayed, the walls came down.

Over every nation is assigned enemy principalities, and powers and spiritual wickedness in the heavenlies or spiritual atmosphere. They are there to build, protect, and promote Satan's dominion in the Earth. Satan is called the prince of the power of the air.

We see this demonstrated in the book of Daniel. For three weeks Daniel had sought the Lord in prayer and fasting for his nation. Finally a messenger arrived. The delay was, he said, because "the prince of the kingdom of Persia withstood me" (Daniel 10:14), i.e., the demon prince over Persia tried to prevent him. Michael the archangel had to come to his assistance. While Daniel was praying, a battle was being fought in the spiritual realm. Daniel's prayers empowered the messenger from God to break through the enemy's blockade.

In Isaiah 25:7 this blockade is called a veil, or a covering, over all people: *"And He will destroy on this mountain the surface of the covering cast over all people, and the veil that is spread over all nations."* This "mountain" refers to Mount Zion and stands for the people of God. Through His people God is going to destroy the covering or the veil which the enemy has cast over all people and all nations. It is this veil which brings spiritual blindness over the people of the Earth.

> *But even if our gospel is veiled, it is veiled to those who are perishing, whose minds the god of this age has blinded, who do not believe, lest the light of the gospel of the glory of Christ, who is the image of God, should shine on them. (2 Corinthians 4:3, 4)*

As we pray, we are causing the veil to be destroyed. Who would knowingly choose eternal death rather than eternal life? What person, in full knowledge of the truth, would turn his back on the love of God in Christ Jesus? Though they don't yet realize it, He is the fulfillment of all their longings. Jesus came to bear witness to the truth and open the eyes of the blind. At the Cross He prayed, "Father forgive them, for they know not what they do." He has compassion for the people of the world in their blindness. His Church is to continue the work of bringing light and sight to the world.

"I, the LORD, have called you in righteousness,

And will hold Your hand;

I will keep You and give You as a covenant to the people,

As a light to the Gentiles,

To open blind eyes,

To bring out prisoners from the prison,

Those who sit in darkness from the prison house." (Isaiah 42:6, 7)

God loves all people; Jesus died for all people; the work of reconciliation has been done for all people. The early Church at first thought that the gospel was for the Jews only. God expanded their vision to show that the Cross included everyone. He showed the apostle Peter a sheet let down from Heaven filled with all kinds of animals considered unclean under the Law and said, *"Rise, Peter, kill and eat."* Peter refused, saying, *"Not so, Lord! For I have never eaten anything common or unclean."* God replied, *"What God has cleansed you must not call common"* (Acts 10:9–17; emphasis added). The cleansing, reconciling work has already been done for all people, but it is hidden by the veil of spiritual blindness spread over all nations.

There is an increasing number of accounts of Muslims coming to Christ, sometimes whole communities, through dreams and visions. This is, I believe, the result of the growing awareness of Christians of the need to pray for Islamic people. Apart from the prayers going up every day, millions of Christians around the globe join in prayer through Ramadan for the Muslim world. The covering or veil over those nations needs to be torn, or, to use the language of the type, the wall has to be brought down. It may look like an impregnable stronghold but our Code shows us that it can be done. Every obstacle will be destroyed that stands in the way of the advancing Army of God as it moves to possess the Earth for the Kingdom.

A missionary friend told me of one occasion when her team had put in much prayer for a certain country in Africa. Shortly after that they went to evangelize there. One town was directly on the border, with the boundary line passing through a street. On one side of the street, the side in the country that was the object of prayer, the people were very receptive to the gospel; on the other side there was little response. The battle in the heavenlies prepares the way for the proclamation of the gospel. Every Christian can and must be involved in this battle. We can all be part of changing the spiritual atmosphere over our Earth. In prayer we can set people free from spiritual blindness.

A priority prayer is to pray for Israel. Jesus said He would come again when the people of Israel would welcome Him (Matthew 23:37–39). The number of Messianic Jews increases day by day as we pray. Paul confidently states in Romans 11:26, *"And so all Israel will be saved...."*

God wants whole nations to be saved. He says to the Son and therefore to us, *"Ask of Me, and I will give You the nations for Your inheritance, And the ends of the earth for Your possession"* (Psalm 2:8).

Uganda and Vanuatu are two nations which have been dedicated to the Lord by their governments. Haiti has been dedicated to Satan. He can't have it! The Church of Jesus Christ can and must claim all the nations for Him. [Following the recent earthquake in Haiti there was an overwhelming response to the President's call for a day of prayer. That response is escalating as the Church prays and ministers]

God's people are called to fight a spiritual battle and God is very much involved. Near the walls of Jericho, Joshua was met by the Commander of the Army of the Lord with drawn sword. The hosts of heaven were ready to join the fray. The Heavenly Army doesn't fight <u>for</u> us, they fight <u>with</u> us as we move into the will of God. Man initiates the action in the Earth. Angels aren't authorized to do that. God told Joshua, *"See! I have given Jericho into your hand, its king, and the mighty men of valor"* (Joshua 6:2).

The march around Jericho was soon to begin and the walls of Jericho must fall.

The Enemy, a Defeated Foe

Before they had crossed the Jordan, Joshua sent two spies to spy out the Land, "especially Jericho." When they returned they brought their report to Joshua: *"Truly the LORD has delivered all the land into our hands, for indeed all the inhabitants of the country are fainthearted because of us"* (Joshua 2:24).

Joshua himself, along with Caleb, had brought back a similar report thirty-eight years before, when they went with ten others to spy out the land. Their report of the enemy was that *"their protection has departed from them, and the LORD is with us. Do not fear them"* (Numbers 14:9).

Fear of the giants had kept Israel in the wilderness for many years when all the while the inhabitants of the Land were a defeated foe who were waiting in fear and trembling, dreading the advance of the army of the Lord. Listen to what one inhabitant of the Land had to say:

> *"I know that the LORD has given you the land, that the terror of you has fallen on us, and that all the inhabitants of the land are fainthearted because of you.*
>
> *For we have heard how the LORD dried up the water of the Red Sea for you when you came out of Egypt, and what you did to the two kings of the Amorites who were on the other side of the Jordan, Sihon and Og, whom you utterly destroyed.*
>
> *And as soon as we heard these things, our hearts melted; neither did there remain any more courage in anyone because of you, for the LORD your God, He is God in heaven above and on earth beneath." (Joshua 2:9–11)*

The deliverance of Israel from Egypt set the Canaanites trembling. The Exodus from Egypt and the events of the first Passover, as we have seen, prefigure the Cross and the Resurrection. Since that time the enemy knows he is a defeated foe. He has but two powers left—to accuse and to deceive (Revelation 12:9,10)—and he has used these to the utmost to retain his grip on the Earth.

As Israel wandered around in the wilderness the enemy must have relaxed a little. For a long time Satan had little to fear from the Church as it went into decline. But one day God said to Israel, *"You have skirted this mountain long enough; turn northward"* (Deuteronomy 2:3). Israel was on the move again. The Canaanites heard the news of the victories on the other side of the Jordan and their fear mounted. How terrified they must have been when the Army of God finally crossed the River.

Satan knows that he can't hold out against the Church of God when it advances. Since the Cross, he has no legal rights in the Earth. He retains power only by deceit and accusation. The Cross was a legal transaction. As long as Satan could accuse Man, he retained dominion over the Earth. Through the Law God gathered together all possible grounds of accusation and dealt with them once and for all. Jesus taught that the Law included even our thoughts and attitudes. The Law demanded our death. Christ's vicarious death and resurrection set us free. The Cross satisfied all the legal demands of the Law and thus removed Satan's dominion over us.

> *For I through the law died to the law that I might live to God. I have been crucified with Christ... (Galatians 2:19, 20)*

> *...we do not yet see all things under him [Man]. But we see Jesus, who was made a little lower than the angels, for the suffering of death, crowned with glory and honor, that He, by the grace of God, might taste death for everyone. (Hebrews 2:9; emphasis added)*

We do not yet see all things under our feet, but we do see Jesus, our representative, exalted over all things and we can know that our dominion has been restored. Jesus shed His blood for everyone, and on that basis we can challenge Satan's power over the nations. The price was paid for every single person who has ever lived or will live on planet Earth. We can lift up the blood of Jesus over every nation and proclaim Jesus' Lordship. At the name of Jesus, every knee is going to bow and every tongue is going to confess His rightful rule over the Earth. In His mighty Resurrection, the Lord of the Church served an eviction notice on the hordes of hell. The time has come for the Church to enforce it.

In the book of 1 Samuel, chapter 30 there is a story which illustrates what God is going to do in the Earth. David and his men had been away from their camp in Ziklag and returned to find that their families and their possessions had been taken by the Amalekites. Though weary and dispirited, David and some of his men pursued the enemy and recovered all. Verse 19 records: *"And nothing of theirs was lacking, either small or great, sons or daughters, spoil or anything which they had taken from them; David recovered all"* (1 Samuel 30:19; emphasis added).

God didn't let the enemy get away with anything. Do we think that He's going to let Satan steal the Earth?

Jericho, the first and strongest city, was the key to conquering the Land. It typifies Satan's rule over the Kingdoms of this world. The conquest of Jericho gives us vital clues as to how to take nations for the Kingdom of God. In all of this we need to remember that we are not wrestling against flesh and blood, against people, but against the spiritual powers of darkness. Our aim is to set people free to see truth and receive the Gospel.

Satan's domain may look secure, but it is founded on lies and deceit. God's people operating in God's truth will demolish the whole shaky structure. Satan is called "the father of lies." One of the biggest lies he has foisted on mankind is that we are just jumped-up monkeys. As the Bible says, *"For as he* [a man] *thinks in his heart, so is he"* (Proverbs 23:7).

> **Satan's domain may look secure, but it is founded on lies and deceit. God's people operating in God's truth will demolish the whole shaky structure.**

If you believe that you are just an animal, you are inclined to act like one, becoming more and more animalistic in behaviour and delighting the devil by dancing with abandon to his tune. His greatest fear is that we will discover who we really are.

The army that God is raising in the Earth will have their eyes fully opened to see things as God sees them. "Jericho" will fall. There is no fear in the ranks, only the steady, purposeful march around the city.

As in the Book of Revelation, the account of the fall of Jericho contains a lot of sevens, the number of perfection or completion. That is no coincidence because the battle of Jericho is a type of the end-time battle for the world. God is about to wrap things up. There are seven priests with seven trumpets, seven days of circling the city with seven circuits on the seventh day.

The Army is instructed to circle the city for seven days, seven times on the last day. The Ark of the Covenant signifying the Presence of God is in the midst of them, borne by priests. The hosts of Heaven are there also. Seven priests, each blowing a trumpet, are to precede the Ark. This was the only sound to be made. On the last circuit on the last day there is to be a long blast of the trumpets and a loud cry from the people. The usual weapons and tactics of warfare were not evident during the march. This was to be spiritual warfare. The account of the fall of Jericho shows us the nature of the battle and how it will be won. This is a battle for the Kingdoms of this World to become the Kingdoms of our Lord and of His Christ.

The trumpets used were not the silver trumpets used on military occasions or for assembling the people, but were to be *shophars*—trumpets made of ram's horns. It was a ram caught by its horns in a thicket that provided the substitutionary sacrifice for Isaac on Mount Moriah (Genesis 22:13). Shophars were used on special occasions, particularly on the <u>Feast of Trumpets</u> at the beginning of the seventh month which heralded the ten holy days leading up to the <u>Day of Atonement</u> and the final Feast, the <u>Feast of Tabernacles</u>. They were also used to announce the <u>Year of Jubilee</u> beginning on the Great Day of Atonement every fifty years. The shophars were jubilee-horns (from *yobel,* meaning "ram"). Whenever these were blown it was the announcement of the coming of the Kingdom, the end of labour and sorrow and the entrance of God's people into their inheritance. In the Year of Jubilee, all slaves were set free, all debts cancelled, all property was restored, and the Land was to rest (lie fallow).

The Lion Concise Bible Encyclopedia states: "The jubilee law may have proved too difficult to keep, so it was looked forward to as a time that only God could introduce. It was the 'year' promised by Isaiah (61:1–20) and proclaimed by Jesus."

When Jesus returned from the wilderness in the power of the Spirit, He announced Jubilee *"...the acceptable year of the Lord."*

"The Spirit of the LORD is upon Me,

Because He has anointed Me to preach the gospel to the poor,

He has sent Me to heal the brokenhearted,

To preach deliverance to the captives

And recovery of sight to the blind,

To set at liberty those who are oppressed,

To preach the acceptable year of the LORD." (Luke 4:18, 19)

Jesus proclaimed deliverance, liberty, healing, and restoration. He was announcing that the Kingdom of God had come. His whole ministry after that was a demonstration of the rule of the Kingdom.

The voice of the Lord is described as a trumpet at Mount Sinai and in the Book of Revelation. It was as a jubilee trumpet making divine proclamations.

In claiming nations for God, we proclaim Jubilee as we speak God's Word over them and pray God's will for them. When God's people pray and proclaim God's Word in faith, it is as though God Himself is speaking.

"By faith the walls of Jericho fell down after they were encircled for seven days." (Hebrews 11:30)

The Army in its march around Jericho was to keep silent. The only sound was to be the blasts of the shophars. This doesn't mean that in our warfare with the enemy we cannot speak, because faith involves believing in your heart and speaking with your mouth (Romans 10:8, 9), but it is what we speak that matters. It was a negative confession that had kept Israel from possessing the Land thirty-eight years before. Now only God's Voice (Word) was to be heard, not man's.

Blow the trumpet in Zion,

And sound the alarm in My holy mountain!

Let all the inhabitants of the land tremble;

For the day of the LORD is coming,

For it is at hand...

The LORD gives voice before His army,

For His camp is very great;

For strong is the One who executes His word,

For the day of the LORD is great and very terrible;

Who can endure it? (Joel 2:1, 11)

In line with the principle of the code—demonstrated in Israel, fulfilled in Christ, manifested through the Church—we witness:

Jubilee was first announced by Israel in type as they marched around Jericho carrying the Ark of God and blowing the jubilee-horns. The city could not stand against the Presence and the Voice of the Lord as typified by the Ark and blast of the shophar. The walls fell down and Jericho was destroyed. The advent of the kingdom of God means the destruction of His enemies.

Jubilee was proclaimed by Jesus in the synagogue in Nazareth. He demonstrated that the Kingdom of God had come by destroying the works of the devil in deliverance, healing, and proclamation of the Gospel. He then went to the Cross to bring redemption to Man and sent the Holy Spirit to empower His Church.

Jubilee is shortly to be announced by the Church. Whenever the Church has proclaimed the gospel, there has been a measure of Jubilee. But the time of fullness is coming when there will be a complete demolition of the dominion of Satan. All the captives will be set free, all debts cancelled; there will be a restoration of all that Satan has stolen.

When the Church rises up in prayer and proclamation of the Word over the nations, the walls of "Jericho" will fall. Then Jesus' ministry of healing, deliverance, and restoration will be replicated in the Church throughout the world as they demonstrate the rule of the Kingdom. There will be "recovery of sight" to the spiritually blind as the veil over the nations is destroyed. There will be an increasing awareness of the presence of God and the Holy Spirit will intensify His work of convicting and convincing the world. Signs, wonders and healing miracles will accompany the preaching of the Word as the Lord of the Church ministers to and through His Body. Whole nations will come into the Kingdom of God. The gates of Hell will fall before the Church of Jesus Christ. (This is *Elijah* who is to come and restore all things that we considered in Chapter 1.) In the light of all these things what shall we do?

Be consecrated to the task ahead. As we have seen, before Israel crossed the Jordan, Joshua instructed the people to sanctify themselves and be ready for great things. God is about to do unprecedented things in the Earth. His people need to be ready. It is a great privilege to be living in these times and to be part of what God is going to do.

Rise up O Men of God, have done with lesser things,

Give heart and soul and mind and strength, to serve the King of kings.

(The Methodist Hymnbook, hymn 585, William Pearson Merrill)

We are entering into the time of the restoration of all things. We are reaping where others have sown. The people of faith of all ages have looked for and worked toward this great Harvest. In the words of another: "This is our finest hour."

Ask for the Holy Spirit to equip you for the task ahead. We are fighting a spiritual battle and need the wisdom, discernment, and power of the Holy Spirit. If you have not already done so, ask for a spiritual prayer language. It is a mighty weapon. Pray for a personal Pentecost.

Come out of the wilderness of works. If you've been battling the flesh, put your confidence in the one perfect sacrifice made for you and consider that battle won; *"...present yourselves to God as being alive from the dead, and your members as instruments of righteousness to God"* (Romans 6:11–14). Focus on the real battle: against principalities and powers and spiritual wickedness. Let the Holy Spirit correct and guide you, but ignore the condemnations of the Accuser. He is desperate to keep you under. Stand in your position in Christ.

Keep your eyes on the goal. Don't get sidetracked. The Great Commission hasn't changed and will not change in the face of Antichrists, wars and rumors of wars, persecutions, earthquakes or anything else. Never mind looking at the storm. Watch the Ark! We must keep our eyes on Jesus and the goal He has set before us. We have not yet made disciples of all the nations. We are destined to take the world for Christ. Through Israel, God has shown us that it can be done. The Cross of Jesus Christ secures it. There is a battle up ahead, but we will win.

Keep the unity of the Spirit with other members of the true Body of Christ. Though two and a half tribes of Israel wanted to settle on the other side of Jordan, God said that their warriors were to go into the Land and fight with the rest. We have a common Lord, a common enemy, and a common goal. Standing together we will prevail. Develop your own ministry and encourage others.

Occupy. Jesus instructed, "Occupy till I come" (Luke 19:13). This is God's world! Stay involved. In the past, many Christians have pursued a policy of non-involvement and created a vacuum which has been filled by others with worldly agendas. God needs Christian politicians, educators, medical people, business, agricultural, and industrial people, judicial people, labourers, scientists, housewives, union officials, etc., working to see that the principles of the Kingdom of God are applied in our world. Don't leave the administration of our world to the enemy. It is inconsistent to pray that God's will be done on Earth as it is in Heaven and then do nothing to help ensure that it is.

Above all, PRAY. Ask God what nation/s He would have you pray for. Your own nation, no doubt, and also Israel (in obedience to Psalm 122:6), then one or more other nations. This is something every one of us can do. Be confident that you are not alone. God is calling hundreds, thousands, maybe millions of others to pray for those nations also. Begin your Jericho march around these nations claiming them for God. Know that the heavenly hosts are fighting with you.

Ask God for that nation for the Kingdom. Remind Him of the promise in Psalm 2:8: *"Ask of Me, and I will give You the nations for Your inheritance, And the ends of the earth for Your possession."* As a member of the Body of Christ, this is a promise to you.

Proclaim the Word of God over the nation/s. Proclaim that Jesus is Lord over that nation and every knee will bow to Him and every tongue will confess that He is Lord. Proclaim the victory won at the Cross. Thank God that He loves every person in that nation and is not willing that any one of them should perish. Lift up the Blood of Jesus shed for every person in that nation and proclaim that the ransom has been paid for every one of them. Tell Satan that the Blood is against him and he is defeated. Pray for the rending of the veil over that nation. Pray for eyes to be opened to truth. Pray for dreams and visions of Jesus for the people of that nation.

Pray for the Christians in that nation. Pray for their safety if they are in a nation hostile to the gospel. Pray for the building up of the Church there. Pray for signs and wonders to be done in the name of Jesus and especially for healing miracles. Pray for an ongoing vision for the Church and unity among Christians. Pray that God's name be honoured, His will be done, and His Kingdom come in that nation as it is in Heaven.

Pray for the "Sauls" to be turned into "Pauls." The Holy Spirit is well able to go right into terrorist camps and organizations with His convicting and convincing power. He's done it before and is still doing it.

Pray for any other specifics known to you and as led by the Spirit. Pray with the understanding and with the spirit. Jesus taught that the priority prayer must be that God's name be honoured, His will be done, and His Kingdom come on the Earth as it is in Heaven. There will no doubt be many personal matters for which we need to pray but if we seek the Kingdom first, God will look after us and our needs.

Be consistent and persistent. As the Army marched around Jericho every day, there wasn't one single crack, no sign that the walls would fall, but fall they did—at the end of the seventh circuit on the seventh day. Suppose that they had given up on the sixth day? We know, and the devil knows, that it's only a matter of time; but we must continue to the end. Be confident that things are happening in the spiritual realms as we pray. The answer may manifest as suddenly as the walls of Jericho fell.

Soon the loud cry will arise:

The kingdoms of this world have become the kingdoms of our Lord and of His Christ, and He shall reign forever and ever! (Revelation 11:15)

And

Now salvation, and strength, and the kingdom of our God, and the power of His Christ have come, for the accuser of our brethren, who accused them before our God day and night, has been cast down.

And they overcame him by the blood of the Lamb and by the word of their testimony, and they did not love their lives to the death. (Revelation 12:10, 11)

Chapter 13. The Birth of the Overcomers

If someone were to have written a book in the first century BC saying that Messiah would be virgin-born to a peasant couple in Bethlehem; that he would grow up to be a humble carpenter in Nazareth; that He would be put to death on a Cross, be resurrected, and taken up to heaven leaving a little band of followers, it wouldn't have gotten a lot of press. Everyone "knew" that Messiah would come as a mighty conqueror, end the Roman occupation, and restore the glory of Israel. They had it all worked out. Yet the real story was there in the Scriptures.

Not many on Earth were aware of His coming into the world—a young betrothed couple, an elderly lady called Elizabeth and the babe she was carrying, some wise men, and some shepherds. There was also a man called Simeon and an old prophetess called Anna, devout people who spent much time in the temple. When the heavenly Babe was brought to the temple to be dedicated, they recognized Him and gave thanks to God. They had been waiting for the birth of this special Babe. The Holy Spirit had revealed to Simeon that he would not see death before he had seen the Lord's Christ. He took Jesus into his arms and blessed God and said, *"Lord, now You are letting Your servant depart in peace, According to Your word; For my eyes have seen Your salvation"* (Luke 2:29, 30).

There are some Annas and Simeons today who are waiting for, and will see, the birth of a special Child. This birth is recorded in Revelation 12. John describes the *"great sign"* in heaven. He sees a woman clothed with the sun, with the moon under her feet. Her head is garlanded with twelve stars. She is ready to give birth. A great fiery red dragon stands by, ready to devour the Child as soon as it is born. He draws a third of the stars of heaven (angels) to follow him. The Child, a male Child, is destined to rule all nations and is caught up to the throne of God as soon as He is born. The result is war in Heaven—Michael and his angels against the dragon and his angels—with the heavenly hosts victorious. The dragon and his angels are cast down. There is no mystery about the identity of the dragon. He is *"that serpent of old, called the Devil and Satan, who deceives the whole world"* (Revelation 12:9).

> **There are some Annas and Simeons today who are waiting for, and will see, the birth of a special Child.**

The Woman has been understood to be Israel, the twelve stars being the twelve tribes; the Child, Christ. This is certainly a valid and obvious interpretation. Jesus is the One Who is born to rule and only through the Cross can Satan be defeated. However, there could be more to the mystery than this obvious answer. Let us see if the code can add to our understanding of the vision.

At the beginning, when Man fell, God said to the serpent:

"And I will put enmity between you and the woman,

And between your seed and her Seed;

He shall bruise your head,

And you shall bruise His heel." (Genesis 3:15)

The Seed of the Woman is destined to crush the serpent's head. The Seed of the Woman is an overcomer who will conqueror the enemy. God told Father Abraham, *"Thy seed shall possess the gate of his enemies"* (Genesis 22:17 KJV). There are not two "Seeds"; the Seed of the Woman and the Seed of Abraham are one and the same.

The Seed is one but many. In Galatians 3:16 Paul says that Abraham's Seed is Christ but he goes on to say in verse 29, *"And if you are Christ's, then you are Abraham's seed and heirs according to the promise."* As in the principle of the Code, the Seed was:

Demonstrated in Israel. [The Corporate Son]God told Abraham and *"In Isaac your seed shall be called"* Genesis 21:12 Abraham's natural Seed which sprang from Isaac, was the many-membered nation of Israel whom God called His Son. The battle in the heavenlies depicted in Revelation 12 was previewed in type in Israel when Abraham's Seed, under Joshua, possessed the gate of his enemies in the fall of Jericho. The ultimate deliverance and victory were yet to come.

Fulfilled in Christ. [The Only Begotten Son] Jesus is the One Who makes it all possible. His is the victory and His is the glory. His triumph over Death and Hell has become ours.

"Worthy is the Lamb who was slain

To receive power and riches and wisdom,

And strength and honor and glory and blessing!" (Revelation 5:12)

"For You were slain, and have redeemed us to God by Your blood

Out of every tribe and tongue and people and nation,

And have made us kings and priests to our God;

And we shall reign on the earth." (Revelation 5:9)

However, that victory has yet to be:

<u>Manifested through the Church</u>. [The Corporate Spiritual Son] The Woman in Revelation 12 is the people of faith of all the ages. Many women in the Bible tell us something about this Woman—Eve, Rahab, Rachel, Rebekah, Ruth, Mary. However, she is best represented by Sarah, Abraham's wife, because this is an ancient woman. She has been travailing for a long time to bring forth the promised Seed—ever since the promise of a Deliverer made in Eden. Just as Sarah was made beautiful and fruitful in her old age, so the Church will be renewed in these last days and she will bring forth the overcoming Seed.

The dragon is standing by, waiting to devour the Child. Satan knows that the Seed will come who will be his downfall, therefore he has persecuted the people of God down through the ages. Whenever a Deliverer was to be born, the birth was accompanied by the slaughter of innocent children in a desperate attempt to abort the birth. At the time of Moses, Pharaoh, Satan's instrument, commanded all the boy babies to be killed. When Jesus was born, King Herod, the dragon's dupe of the day, ordered the slaughter of all the male children under two.

The coming of a Deliverer is always accompanied by a slaughter of innocents. We are living in a time when millions of babies are being aborted. Could it be that the dragon knows that the time has come for another Deliverer to be born?

The Child is a company of people referred to as "they" in verse 11. It is the generation of Overcomers—the Joshua generation, the product of the ages-long travail of the people of God. Christ is the Head of this company just as He is Head of the Church.

The Child is born and immediately caught up to God and to His throne—the Overcomers rise up in kingdom authority and begin to exercise dominion. The angels join the warfare as they did at Jericho. Satan is cast down.

We have a preview of this in Luke 10. Jesus has sent out seventy disciples on mission. They came back rejoicing that even the demons were subject to them in Jesus' Name. Jesus said,

"I saw Satan fall like lightning from heaven,

Behold, I give you the authority to trample on serpents and scorpions, and over all the power of the enemy, and nothing shall by any means hurt you..." (Luke 10:18, 19)

When God's people rise up in Kingdom authority in Jesus' Name, the works of the devil are destroyed. All believers have kingdom authority. Our legal position in Christ is that we are all seated in heavenly places in Him (Ephesians 2:6). The end-time Church will manifest that authority in an unprecedented way. In the letters to the seven Churches in Revelation, the Lord of the Church makes promises to "he who overcomes." Again these promises belong to all believers, but the Overcomers come into the fullness of faith and claim them. One of these promises is: *"And he who overcomes, and keeps My works until the end, to him I will give power over the nations"* (Revelation 2:26).

The destiny of the nations is wrested from of the serpent and is in the hands of the Seed of the Woman. *"And the God of peace will crush Satan under your feet shortly..."* (Romans 16:20).

In Revelation 8, the prayers of the saints are the catalyst for apocalyptic happenings on the Earth. Jesus said, in Mark 13, not to be troubled when we hear of wars and rumors of wars or earthquakes or famines, for such things <u>must</u> happen. They are the beginning of sorrows, literally "birth pangs." Something is being birthed in the Earth. It is all part of the end-time battle. God has said that He is going to shake the Earth (Hebrews 12:26–28). He's going to rearrange things a bit. This is God's answer to our prayers. When the dust settles, the

Eternal Kingdom will be clearly established in the Earth and all that is not of that Kingdom will be removed.

Chapter 14. The King Is Coming

He comes! Down from the heights of Mount Olivet, accompanied by His train of attendants, lifting their voices in joyful praise. A multitude comes out from the city to greet Him as is fitting for a king, and the royal procession sweeps into Jerusalem with Hosanna-shouts.

The occasion is Jesus' triumphal entry into Jerusalem at the beginning of that Passover of destiny. He is riding a donkey in fulfillment of a prophecy.

"Rejoice greatly, O daughter of Zion!

Shout, O daughter of Jerusalem!

Behold, your King is coming to you;

He is just and having salvation,

Lowly and riding on a donkey,

A colt, the foal of a donkey...." (Zechariah 9:9)

Jesus was proclaiming and the crowds were acclaiming that He was the Messiah-King. The crowds were also, unknowingly, choosing the

Passover Lamb for the world. His throne would be a Cross and His Crown a crown of thorns and the cheers would turn into jeers in just a few short days.

The whole scene on that memorable first Palm Sunday was fulfillment of so much that had gone before and prophetic of that longed-for day, when the King will come again in triumph to reign on Earth. He will descend from Heaven accompanied by *"ten thousands of His saints"* (Jude 14); just as Jesus in His descent from Mount Olivet was accompanied by His disciples and other pilgrims who were lodging in the nearby villages. The crowds went out from the city to meet the procession as benefits a king and all escorted Him into Jerusalem, so on that day *"...we who are alive and remain shall be caught up together with them in the clouds to meet the Lord in the air. And thus we shall always be with the Lord"* (1 Thessalonians 4:17).

This is the event commonly known as "The Rapture." As Jesus enters the Earth's atmosphere, decay and death disappear, Creation will be renewed, dead bodies resurrected, and Eden restored. Jesus will be escorted into the city with great joy and seated on the throne of the Kingdom. God promised David, His chosen king, that one of his sons would sit on the throne of the Eternal Kingdom.

> *"He shall build Me a house, and I will establish his throne forever.*
>
> *I will be his Father, and he shall be My son...*
>
> *And I will establish him in My house and in My kingdom forever;*
>
> *and his throne shall be established forever." (1 Chronicles 17:12–14)*

Jesus is, literally, Son of Man and Son of God. In Him Heaven and Earth are joined. When He comes again, Heaven comes with Him.

David had wanted to build a temple for God but he was forbidden because he was a man of war. His son Solomon (meaning "peace") was to build the temple. The Kingdom was established before Solomon came to the throne. Before Jesus, the Prince of Peace, sits on the throne there has to be the time of war. The war which began under Joshua came to an end under David; then came the time of peace and prosperity under Solomon.

Jesus is the Son of David, *"greater than Solomon"* (Matthew 12:42). He has built God a temple, the Church: *"a holy temple," "a habitation of God in the Spirit"* (Ephesians 2:21, 22). Joined together in one Body, we share His Glory.

The climax of Israel's history was when Solomon dedicated the temple and it was filled with the Glory of God. When Jesus sits on the throne of the Earth, the Glory of God will fill the Earth as it was promised long ago.

A Gift for the King

"...and the time came for the saints to possess the kingdom" (Daniel 7:22)

We're getting ready a present for Jesus. It has to be a present fit for the King of kings. What would you be prepared to contribute?

It is said that when Queen Victoria first heard that Jesus would come again she said, "I wish that He would come during my reign so that I could lay my crown at His feet." The Wise Men brought Him gifts of gold, frankincense, and myrrh. A sinful woman brought Him a gift of fragrant oil with tears and kisses for His feet. Joseph gave Him a tomb and a costly burial cloth. Down through the ages, those who glimpsed His worth gave what they could, sometimes their whole life even unto death, and so the Kingdom comes.

Satan offered Him a present once. He offered Him the world—all of its kingdoms, all of its glory, and all the authority that went with it. *"For,"* he boasted, *"it has been delivered to me and I give it to whomever I wish. Therefore, if You will worship before me, all will be Yours"* (Luke 4:6, 7). It was a very real temptation for Jesus. This was the world that He created; these were the people He so loved. Jesus didn't dispute Satan's ownership—Adam had handed it to him—but to possess it on Satan's terms meant that the world was eternally lost. Jesus chose the way of the Cross. He wanted the world free and unsullied as it would be under the rule of the Kingdom of God; a world where there would be no more crying, pain, sorrow, or death.

After the triumph of the Resurrection, Jesus was able to say, *"All authority has been given unto Me in heaven and on earth. Go therefore and make disciples of all the nations..."* (Matthew 28:18, 19; emphasis added). Dominion over the Earth belongs now to the Seed of Abraham and they have it in their power to release the Earth from the grip of the usurper. The ransom has been paid for every man, woman, and child in every nation, but so many of them live in the darkness of the devil's deceit.

Perhaps you are one who doesn't give too much thought about people in the rest of the world. You may be prepared to pray fervently for your own family and friends and even your own nation, and so we should. But Jesus loves everybody. He longs for them, no matter who they are or what they've done. "Forgive them Father for they know not what they do."

On the journey into Jerusalem that Palm Sunday, he wept over the city.

> "O Jerusalem, Jerusalem, the one who kills the prophets and stones those who are sent to her! How often I wanted to gather your children together, as a hen gathers her chicks under her wings, but you were not willing!" (Matthew 23:37)

It is the cry of His heart for every city, every nation, every person. If we really love Jesus we will want to give Him the desire of His heart. Together we can do it! We have the promise:

> "Ask of Me, and I will give You
>
> The nations for Your inheritance,
>
> And the ends of the earth for Your possession." (Psalm 2:8)

Yes, we're getting ready a present for the King. He's going to love it. He's going to say, "Just what I always wanted." What are you prepared to contribute?

> Then to Him was given dominion and glory and a kingdom,
>
> That all peoples, nations, and languages should serve Him.
>
> His dominion is an everlasting dominion,
>
> Which shall not pass away,

And His kingdom the one

Which shall not pass away. (Daniel 7:14)

AMEN, COME LORD JESUS!

Summary

Israel is a sign. Through Abraham and the nation which came from him, God revealed His plan for regaining the Earth for the Kingdom: -

A Father would offer up His Son on the Mountains of Moriah. This Son will have been born through the miraculous intervention of God. Through this Son will come a people who are destined to recover a lost inheritance. He will call this nation His Son. He will redeem them, provide for them, protect them, empower them, teach them and lead them into His purposes. A generation will arise which will enter into those purposes. They will prevail over the enemy, possess the Earth and establish the Kingdom. Then *"all the earth shall be filled with the glory of the Lord."* Numbers 14:21

It will be a quick work. That generation is here and these are those times!

About the Author.

Val lives with her husband Rob on their property north of Mackay, Queensland, Australia. They are retired Pastors. Val has been a keen student of the Bible for about forty years especially in the area of Typology. She has written "The Fall of the Gates of Hell" and also a booklet called "The True Sabbath." She plans to continue writing. In her spare time Val likes to read and garden. Your feedback is welcomed. email vrvpym77@hotmail.com